Ontario Police OACP Prep

SSPO Study Guide Featuring 100s of Practice Questions, Fitness Tracking, and Social Media Strategy

COMPLETE
Test Preparation Inc.
WWW.TEST-PREPARATION.CA

Copyright © 2025 Complete Test Preparation Inc. All Rights Reserved.

Intellectual Property Rights This publication is protected by copyright. No part of this book may be reproduced, copied, distributed, or transmitted in any form or by any means—including graphic, electronic, or mechanical methods such as photocopying, recording, or information storage and retrieval systems—without the prior written permission of the publisher, except in the case of brief quotations embodied in critical reviews and certain other noncommercial uses permitted by copyright law.

Disclaimer & Limitation of Liability While the publisher and author have used their best efforts in preparing this book, they make no representations or warranties with respect to the accuracy or completeness of the contents. The advice and strategies contained herein may not be suitable for your situation. Test content and administration rules change frequently; readers are advised to verify all information with the official test providers. Complete Test Preparation Inc. shall not be liable for any loss of profit or any other commercial damages, including but not limited to special, incidental, consequential, or other damages.

Non-Affiliation Notice Complete Test Preparation Inc. is an independent publisher and is not affiliated with, endorsed by, or sponsored by any testing organization, educational institution, or government agency mentioned in this publication. All trademarks, service marks, and trade names are the property of their respective owners and are used for reference and identification purposes only.

Complete Test Preparation Inc. is not affiliated with the Ontario Police or the Ontario Ministry of Correctional Services, who were not involved in the production of, and do not endorse this product.

We strongly recommend that students check with exam providers for up-to-date information regarding test content.

Provided for Skill Practice Only

ISBN-13: 9781772455212

Version 10 December 2025

Published by
Complete Test Preparation Inc.
Visit us on the web at https://www.test-preparation.ca
Printed in the USA

About Complete Test Preparation Inc.

Why Choose Complete Test Preparation? You want to spend your valuable study time where it counts the most. We've got you covered.

Since 2005, we have helped hundreds of thousands of students succeed with over 145 study guides and online courses. We know that tests change, which is why we keep our content current and relevant.

Study with a Purpose With this purchase, you are doing more than just preparing for a test. You are supporting a mission to improve education globally. We are proud to support charities that bring learning opportunities to those who need them most.

Learn more about our mission:
https://www.test-preparation.ca/charities-and-non-profits/

You have definitely come to the right place.
If you want to spend your valuable study time where it will help you the most - we've got you covered today and tomorrow.

Thank you for studying with us!

Feedback

We welcome your feedback. Email us at feedback@test-preparation.ca with your comments and suggestions. We carefully review all suggestions and often incorporate reader suggestions into upcoming versions. As a Print on Demand Publisher, we update our products frequently.

CONTENTS

6 Getting Started
How this study guide is organized — 8
The Police Constable Study Plan — 9
OACP SIGMA Study Plan & Assessment — 11
Part 1: The Self-Assessment — 11
Part 2: The 3-Week Custom Plan — 12
Part 3: General Study Tips for the SIGMA — 16
Tips for making a schedule — 17

18 Section A Incident Report Writing
Part 1 - Spelling — 19
Spelling Self Assessment — 21
Answer Key and Explanations — 23
Part 2 - Vocabulary — 29
Vocabulary Self Assessment — 30
Answer Key and Explanation — 32
Police Vocabulary Hit List — 33
1. The "Problem Pairs" Confusing Words — 33
2. Essential Police Jargon SSPO Vocabulary — 35
3. The "Double-Letter" Trap List — 38
Part 3 - Grammar and Punctuation — 39
Grammar Punctuation Self-Assessment — 39
Answer Key and Explanation — 43

45 Section B: Police Problem Solving
Part 1 - Rule Following — 46
Rule Following Self-Assessment — 47
Answer Key and Explanations — 50
Map Reading & Directional Logic: — 52
Mapping Self-Assessment — 52
Answer Key and Explanations — 57
Ethical Judgment — 58
Ethical Judgment Self-Assessment — 58
Answer Key and Explanations — 60

62	**Practice Test Questions 1**	
	Answer Key and Explanation	98
115	**Practice Test Questions 2**	
	Answer Key and Explanations	151
167	**OACP Certificate Specifics**	
	Personality Assessment ESQ2 / Sigma	167
	The Structure of the Test	168
	Sample Personality Questions & Analysis	171
	Summary Checklist for Candidates	171
174	**The 14-Day Fitness Log**	
	Rules for the Fitness Log	175
	How to Fill Out the Log	176
	Sample Entries: Good vs. Bad	177
	Common Questions	178
180	**Medical Standards**	
184	**The Social Media Audit**	
	Summary	188
189	**Conclusion**	
190	**Online Resources**	

Getting Started

Welcome to the First Step of Your Future. You have set a goal to enter the Ontario Police, and this test is the gateway. But you shouldn't just aim to take the test—you should aim to crush it.

Getting a high score opens doors. It proves to employers and unions that you have the discipline and the aptitude for the job. Yes, studying requires dedication, but if you focus your energy now, you will soon be holding that acceptance letter.

Where do you start? Right here. It is normal to feel unsure of how to prepare. That's where we come in. This guide maps out everything you need to know, boosting your competency and your confidence.

The Ontario Police Constable Test

Section A – Incident Report Writing

This section tests if you have the literacy skills to write reports, which often are used in court. It may look easy, but tricky spelling and grammar traps can ruin your score.

Spelling

You are given a word (e.g., "Occurance") and must decide YES or NO if it is spelled correctly. Tip: Watch for double letters!

Vocabulary

Choose the best synonym for a word used in a police context (e.g., "The suspect was apprehended").

Grammar & Punctuation

You see 4 versions of a sentence. You must pick the one with correct capitalization and punctuation.

Why Practice Matters You cannot rely on 'gut feeling' for grammar. You need to know the rules of comma splices, capitalization, and subject-verb agreement.

Section B – Police Problem Solving (The "Score Killer")

This section measures your logical reasoning and judgment. It uses realistic police scenarios and map-based questions.

Applying Rules

You are given a rule (e.g., "Officers may only enter a park after dusk if…") and a scenario. You must decide if the officer's action was correct.

Map Reading & Logic

Officer A is 3 blocks north of the bank. Officer B is 2 blocks east…" Questions require spatial orientation and quick mental mapping.

Ethical Judgment and Applying Rules

Determining the "best" course of action in a difficult situation.

While we seek to make our guide as comprehensive as possible, note that like all exams, the Ontario Police Constable test might be adjusted at some future point. New material might be added, or content that is no longer relevant or applicable might be removed. It is always a good idea to give the materials you receive when you register to take the Ontario Police Constable test a careful review.

How This Study Guide is Organized

This study guide is divided into three sections. The first section, Self-Assessments, which will help you recognize your areas of strength and weaknesses. This will be a boon when it comes to managing your study time the most efficiently; there is not much point of focusing on material you have already got firmly under control. Instead, taking the self-assessments will show you where that time could be much better spent. In this area you will begin with a few questions to evaluate quickly your understanding of material that is likely to appear on the test. If you do poorly in certain areas, simply work carefully through those sections in the tutorials and then try the self-assessment again.

The second section, Tutorials, offers information in each of the content areas, as well as strategies to help you master that material. The tutorials are not intended to be a complete course, but cover general principles. If you find that you do not understand the tutorials, it is recommended that you seek out additional instruction.

Third, we offer two sets of practice test questions, similar to those on the exam.

The Police Constable Study Plan

Now that you have made the decision to take the Police Constable test, it is time to get started. Before you do another thing, you will need to figure out a plan of attack. The best study tip is to start early! The longer the time period you devote to regular study practice, the likelier you will be to retain the material and be able to access it quickly. If you thought that 1 x 20 is the same as 2 x 10, guess what? It really is not, when it comes to study time. Reviewing material for just an hour per day over the course of 20 days is far better than studying for two hours a day for only 10 days. The more often you revisit a particular piece of information, the better you will know it. Not only will your grasp and understanding be better, but your ability to reach into your brain and quickly and efficiently pull out the tidbit you need, will be greatly enhanced as well.

The great Chinese scholar and philosopher Confucius believed that true knowledge could be defined as knowing what you know and what you do not know. The first step in preparing for the Police Constable test is to assess your strengths and weaknesses. You may already have an idea of what you know and what you do not know, but evaluating yourself using our Self- Assessment modules for each of the test content areas.

Making a Study Schedule

To make your study time the most productive you will need to develop a study plan. The purpose of the plan is to organize all the bits of pieces of information in such a way that you will not feel overwhelmed. Rome was not built in a day, and learning everything you will need to know to pass the Police Constable is going to take time, too. Arranging the material you need to learn into manageable chunks is the best way to go. Each study session should make you feel as though you have accomplished your goal, or at least are closer, and your goal is simply to learn what you planned to learn during that particular session. Try to organize the content in such a way that each study session builds on previous ones. That way, you will retain the information, be better able to access it, and review the previous bits and pieces at the same time.

Self-assessment

The Best Study Tip! The best study tip is to start early! The longer you study regularly, the more you will retain and 'learn' the material. Studying for 1 hour per day for 20 days is far better than studying for 2 hours for 10 days.

OACP SIGMA Study Plan & Assessment

Part 1: The Self-Assessment

Instructions: Before starting your study journey, rate your current confidence level for each section of the SIGMA Survey on a scale of 1 to 5.

Rating Scale:

1 = I have no idea how to do this.

2 = I struggle often and guess frequently.

3 = I get it right about 50% of the time.

4 = I am confident but make careless errors.

5 = I can teach this to someone else.

SIGMA Test Section	Your Rating (1-5)	Notes / Specific Struggles
Incident Report Writing		
Spelling & Vocabulary		e.g., tough words, homophones (there/their)
Grammar & Punctuation		e.g., sentence fragments, comma usage
Problem Solving		
Basic Math (Arithmetic)		e.g., fractions, decimals, percentages
Following Rules		
Other Skills		
Map Reading / Directions		e.g., following routes, cardinal directions
Ethical Judgment		knowing the "best" vs "neutral" response

PART 2: THE 3-WEEK CUSTOM PLAN

Hypothetical Student Profile Used for This Schedule:

Name: "Candidate Alex"

Assessment Results:

Spelling/Grammar: 2/5 (Weak) – Needs heavy review.

Math/Logic: 2/5 (Weak) – Struggles with fractions and patterns.

Map Reading: 4/5 (Strong) – Needs maintenance only.

Ethics: 5/5 (Very Strong) – Needs minimal review.

WEEK 1: FOUNDATION & WEAKNESS ATTACK

Goal: Re-learn the rules of grammar and math. No timers yet—focus on accuracy.

Day	Focus	Activity
Day 1	Diagnostic	Take a full, un-timed Diagnostic Practice Test to set a baseline score.
Day 2	Spelling	Review the "Top 100 Police Misspelled Words." Create flashcards for words you missed.
Day 3	Math Basics	Focus on Decimals and Fractions. Do 20 practice problems without a calculator.
Day 4	Grammar	Study "Subject-Verb Agreement" and "Sentence Fragments." Fix 10 broken sentences.
Day 5	Rule Following	Review practice scenarios and consider best course of action
Day 6	Review	Re-do the questions you got wrong on Day 1. Did you get them right this time?
Day 7	Rest	Active Recovery:

WEEK 2: APPLICATION & SPEED

Goal: Apply the rules to exam-style questions. Introduce mild time pressure.

Day	Focus	Activity
Day 8	Report Writing	Timed Exercise: Read a sample police scenario and find the 5 grammar errors in 3 minutes.
Day 9	Math & Percents	Word Problems involving money and percentages (e.g., tax, discounts). Time limit: 1 min per question.
Day 10	Map Reading	Complete 3 Map scenarios. Focus on "Cardinal Directions" (North, South, East, West).
Day 11	Vocabulary	Drill yourself on Police Vocabulary
Day 12	Problem Solving	Mixed Math/Logic set. 30 questions in 45 minutes.
Day 13	Ethics	Review 5 ethical scenarios. Write down why the correct answer is correct (justify your logic).
Day 14	Rest	Active Recovery: 30-minute swim or bike ride.

Week 3: Simulation & Mastery

Goal: Simulate the stress of test day. Build mental endurance.

Day	Focus	Activity
Day 15	Full Simulation	Practice Test A: Full length, strictly timed. No phone, no distractions.
Day 16	Analysis	Review Day 15 results. Identify the exact reason for every error (e.g., "Misread question" vs. "Didn't know math").
Day 17	Rapid Fire	50 Spelling/Grammar questions in 20 minutes. Speed drill.
Day 18	Rapid Fire	20 Math Word Problems in 25 minutes. Speed drill.
Day 19	Final Polish	Review your "Problem Areas" list. Re-read the rules for your weakest section.
Day 20	Light Review	Do 10 easy questions to build confidence. Pack your bag for test day (ID, water, pencils).
Day 21	TEST DAY	You are ready. Trust your preparation.

Part 3: General Study Tips for the SIGMA

1. Simulate the Environment
Don't study on your bed. Sit at a hard desk, remove your phone from the room, and use a timer. The SIGMA is stressful because of the clock, not just the content. You need to get used to the pressure.

2. The "Why" Method
When you get a question wrong, don't just look at the right answer and move on. Ask: "Why did I pick the wrong one?"

- Did I rush?
- Did I not know the vocabulary word?
- Did I make a calculation error?
- Fix the root cause, not just the symptom.

3. No Calculator Math
The SIGMA generally does not allow calculators. You must practice doing long division and multiplication by hand on scratch paper. If you practice with a calculator, you will freeze on test day.

4. Read More to Write Better
To improve your grammar and spelling naturally, read high-quality news articles (e.g., CBC News, The Globe and Mail) for 15 minutes a day. Pay attention to how they structure sentences.

5. Don't Ignore the Fitness Log
Use your "Rest Days" in this study plan to fill out your 14-Day Fitness Log. If you fail to submit the log, your high test score won't matter!

Tips for Making a Schedule

Once you make a schedule, stick with it! Make your study sessions reasonable. If you make a study schedule and don't stick with it, you set yourself up for failure. Instead, schedule study sessions that are a bit shorter and set yourself up for success! Make sure your study sessions are do-able. Studying is hard work, but after you pass, you can party and take a break!

Schedule breaks. Breaks are just as important as study time. Work out a rotation of studying and breaks that works for you.

Build up study time. If you find it hard to sit still and study for 1 hour straight through, build up to it. Start with 20 minutes, and then take a break. Once you get used to 20-minute study sessions, increase the time to 30 minutes. Gradually work you way up to 1 hour.

How to Make a Study Plan and Schedule

40 minutes to 1 hour is optimal. Studying for longer than this is tiring and not productive. Studying for shorter isn't long enough to be productive.

Studying Math. Studying Math is different from studying other subjects because you use a different part of your brain. The best way to study math is to practice everyday. This will train your mind to think in a mathematical way. If you miss a day or days, the mathematical mind-set is gone, and you have to start all over again to build it up.

More on how to study math
https://www.test-preparation.ca/study-math/

Flash Cards - The Complete Guide
https://www.test-preparation.ca/flash-cards/

SECTION A
INCIDENT
REPORT
WRITING

Part 1 - Spelling

Why Details Matter in Law Enforcement
You might be asking yourself: "I want to catch criminals and help the community—why does it matter if I can spell 'Lieutenant' or 'Occurrence'?"

In policing, your notebook and your reports are legal documents. A defense attorney's job is to cast doubt on your credibility. If your incident reports are filled with spelling errors and grammatical mistakes, it suggests a lack of attention to detail. If a judge or jury cannot trust your spelling, they may not trust your testimony.

The Sigma Survey for Police Officers (SSPO) tests this rigorously in Section A: Incident Report Writing. This section is not just an English quiz; it is a test of your professional observation skills.

What to Expect
The SSPO often uses a multiple-choice format designed to trigger "semantic satiation"—where looking at four similar misspellings makes the correct word look wrong. You will encounter:

- The "Double Letter" Traps: Words like Harrassment or Possession.
- The "Silent Letter" Traps: Words like Subpoena or Doubt.
- Professional Terminology: Legal terms you will use daily, such as Affidavit, Defendant, and Acquittal.

A Note on Canadian English
This guide is specifically designed for the Ontario (OACP) and Saskatoon markets. We use Canadian English standards.

We use -ce for nouns (e.g., Offence, Defence).

- We use -our for words like Misdemeanour (though Misdemeanor is becoming common, stick to Canadian standard when given the choice).
- We use -re for words like Manoeuvre.

How to Use This Assessment

Don't rush through these questions. This is a diagnostic tool.

Cover the answers: Try to visualize the correct spelling before looking at the options.

Mark your errors: If you get a word wrong, highlight it. That word is now on your "Hit List" to memorize before test day.

Trust the rule, not your eye: If a word looks "weird," apply the spelling rules provided in the answer key.

Ready to test your accuracy? Let's begin.

Answer Sheet

	A	B	C	D
1	○	○	○	○
2	○	○	○	○
3	○	○	○	○
4	○	○	○	○
5	○	○	○	○
6	○	○	○	○
7	○	○	○	○
8	○	○	○	○
9	○	○	○	○
10	○	○	○	○

Instructions: For each question, select the option that represents the correct spelling.

1. A) Leutenant B) Lieutenent C) Lieutenant D) Leiutenant

2. A) Sergeant B) Sargent C) Sergent D) Sargeant

3. A) Ocurence B) Occurrence C) Occurance D) Occurrance

4. A) Surveillance B) Survelance C) Servailance D) Surveilance

5. A) Accommodate B) Acommodate C) Accammadate D) Accomodate

6. A) Separate B) Seperate C) Sepparate D) Seperat

7. A) Harassment B) Harrassment C) Harrasment D) Harasment

8. A) Definite B) Definit C) Defenate D) Defanite

9. A) Judgment B) Judgment C) Jugement D) Both A and B are accepted in Canada, but B is preferred in legal contexts.

10. A) Subpeona B) Subpoena C) Supena D) Subpena

Answer Key and Explanations

1. C) Lieutenant

Tip: Break it down: Lie - u - tenant. Remember: "You (u) can lie to a tenant."

2. A) Sergeant

Tip: Look for the 'e' in the first syllable and 'a' in the second. Think Ser - geant.

3. B) Occurrence

Tip: Double C, Double R. When a suffix starting with a vowel is added to a stressed syllable ending in a consonant, double the consonant.

4. A) Surveillance

Tip: Sur - veil - lance. Remember the word "Veil" (like a wedding veil) is hidden inside.

5. A) Accommodate

Tip: This word is "greedy"—it wants two of everything. Two Cs, Two Ms.

6. A) Separate

Tip: There is "A Rat" in "Sep-A-RAT-e." Never use 'e' in the middle.

7. A) Harassment

Tip: One R, Two Ss. It comes from the French harasser.

8. A) Definite

Tip: The root word is Finite. It definitely does not have an 'a' in the middle.

9. D) Judgment

Tip: In general Canadian usage, "Judgment" is acceptable, but in Legal contexts (police reports, court documents), the 'e' is dropped: Judgment.

10. B) Subpoena

Spelling Rules

Improving and learning spelling takes time, practice and learning the rules. Understanding the spelling rules and exceptions to the rules is the greatest strategy to help you know how to spell.

Understanding spelling rules is just one of the numerous strategies that can help you spell well.

So if you forget the spelling pattern, maybe you can remember the rules, and you hopefully understand why spelling is the way it is. Many spelling rules can assist you in improving your spelling. Let's look at some of the spelling rules in a basic way:

1. I Before E, Except After C

There are various exceptions to this spelling rule, and it is better to think of it as a spelling guideline. It can be essential to words such as:

I before E
Example: Would you like to eat a piece of cake? Jamal will believe the story. They are planting new crops in the field.

Except before C
Example: Darnell received a trophy in the athletics competition. Nikita spotted a rat on the ceiling.

Unless the vowel sounds like A
Example: Our neighbours stay in a beige cottage. What is the height of the building?

Hint: It is a good idea to remember common exceptions to the spelling rule.

2. Adding Suffixes to Words Ending with Y
When you add a suffix that begins with E such as –ed, -est, or –er to any word ending with Y, the Y often changes to I. For example:

    Fry- Fried
    Dry- Dried-Drier
    Baby- babies
    Ugly – Ugliest

Add –ies if the word has a constant before Y after removing Y. For example:

Daddy- daddies
Difficulty - difficulties
Company – companies

3. Drop the Silent E
Usually, an E after a constant at the end of any word is considered silent; hence, it affects how you pronounce the vowel coming before the constant. The E enables the vowel

sound of the word to be long rather than short. It is critical to understand the silent E correctly because the presence or absence of silent E can change a word's meaning.

Example 1: The dog bit me. Keep your leg out of the cage. The dog's bite

Adding the E at the end of the word bit changes the meaning of the word from past to present.

Example 2: Beware of the sharp knives; you can cut yourself. The man is very cute.

Adding the silent E in the sentence above creates a different word.

When you add a suffix such as -est, -ed, or -er, the silent E is often dropped from the main word's end.

Example: The cat bared his teeth at the child for a long. The kitten's eyes were bluest of all.

You can drop the silent E when you add a vowel suffix at the end of a word.

For example:

Bite – biting
Joke – joking
Opposite + ion = Opposition
Sense + ible = Sensible.

4. Double Consonants
Double consonants are regularly found in words with suffixes.

Example: I dropped the luggage in the car. Daniel called for you.
Some words can be pronounced either as one or two syllables, but their spelling remains the same in a sentence.

Example: Blessed are the humble, for they shall inherit heaven.

In the sentence above is a fixed expression, hence blessed is pronounced as two syllables:
Bless-ed.

Example: The Bishop blessed the couples after their wedding.
In the sentence above, the word blessed is pronounced as one syllable: blest.
Double consonants can change the meanings and pronunciation.

Example: Sisal is native to the desert. Would you like ice tea for dessert?

5. Plural Suffixes
You can add -es when the word ends with -sh, -z, -x, -s, or -ch. For example:
I took one bus to town; you took two buses.

I only made **one wish** to the pastor; you made **two wishes**.
I am unloading **one box** of books; you are unloading the remaining **five boxes**.

Add –s for all other endings. For example:
I drank one cup of tea in the morning; you drank two cups.
I have one pair of a shoe; you bought three pairs of shoes.

6. Changing "-f" to "-s" or "-ves."
Most words that end in "-fe" or "-f" often change their plurals to "-ves." For example:

Wife – wives
Thief – thieves
Leaf – leaves
Knife – knives
Calf – calves

Some of the words end their plurals with "-s" or "-ves." For example:

Handkerchief – handkerchieves or handkerchiefs
Dwarf – dwarves or dwarfs

You can add -s to words that end with -ff to make plural. For example:
Scuff – scuffs
Cliff – cliffs

Add -s to some words that end in -f. Nouns ending in two vowels plus "-f" often form plurals in the usual manner with an "-s" at the end. For example:
Spoof – spoofs
Chief – chiefs
Oaf – oafs.

Part 2 - Vocabulary

Answer Sheet

	A	B	C	D
1	○	○	○	○
2	○	○	○	○
3	○	○	○	○
4	○	○	○	○
5	○	○	○	○
6	○	○	○	○
7	○	○	○	○
8	○	○	○	○
9	○	○	○	○
10	○	○	○	○

Instructions
Read each sentence carefully. Select the word or phrase that best defines the **bolded** word as it is used in the context of the sentence.

1. The officer had to **apprehend** the suspect before he crossed the border.

A) Question B) Arrest C) Release D) Search

2. The witness was able to **corroborate** the victim's time line of events.

A) Contradict B) Confirm C) Write down D) Forget

3. The suspect became **belligerent** when asked for his identification.

A) Confused B) Hostile C) Cooperative D) Silent

4. The defense lawyer argued that his client's difficult childhood should **mitigate** the sentence.

A) Increase B) Cancel C) Lessen D) Explain

5. The driver was found **culpable** for the accident due to his negligence.

A) Blameworthy B) Innocent C) Injured D) Unaware

6. Officers must enforce the **statute** regarding noise complaints after 11:00 PM.

A) Opinion B) Suggestion C) Law D) Warning

7. It is illegal to **coerce** a confession from a detainee.

A) Record B) Force C) Request D) Reject

8. The search revealed a large quantity of **illicit** substances in the vehicle.

A) Illegal B) Imported C) Unknown D) Dangerous

9. New DNA evidence helped to **exonerate** the man who had been in prison for ten years.

A) Convict B) Transfer C) Absolve D) Identify

10. The undercover unit maintained constant **surveillance** on the warehouse.

A) Distance B) Attacks C) Communication D) Observation

Answer Key and Explanation

1. B) Arrest.
Apprehend means to take into custody or arrest someone for a crime.

2. B) Confirm.
Corroborate means to support a statement with evidence or authority.

3. B) Hostile.
Belligerent means hostile and aggressive.

4. C) Lessen.
Mitigate means to make something less severe, serious, or painful.

5. A) Blameworthy.
Culpable means deserving blame. (Think: "Culprit").

6. C) Law.
A statute is a written law passed by a legislative body.

7. B) Force.
Coerce means to persuade (an unwilling person) to do something by using force or threats.

8. A) Illegal.
Illicit means forbidden by law, rules, or custom.

9. C) Absolve.
Exonerate means to clear someone from blame or a criminal charge.

10. D) Observation.
Surveillance is close observation, especially of a suspected spy or criminal.

Police Vocabulary Hit List

The following lists are organized into three study sections. This list contains approximately 80 high-frequency words that are statistically most likely to appear on the SSPO Section A.

1. The "Problem Pairs" Confusing Words

These are the most common traps in the Sentence Editing/Grammar section. The test asks you to choose the correct word for the sentence context.

1. Advice vs. Advise
Advice (Noun): A suggestion or recommendation. ("I need your legal advice.")
Advise (Verb): The act of giving a suggestion. ("I advise you to remain silent.")

2. Effect vs. Affect
Effect (Noun): A result or consequence. ("The alcohol had a visible effect on his driving.")
Affect (Verb): To influence or change. ("The weather did not affect our response time.")

3. Lose vs. Loose
Lose (Verb): To misplace or fail to keep. ("Do not lose your badge.")
Loose (Adjective): Not tight or secure. ("The suspect had a loose grip on the weapon.")

4. Licence vs. License (Canadian Rule)
Licence (Noun): The document. ("Show me your driver's licence.")
License (Verb): The action. (" The city will license the new vendor.")

5. Offence vs. Offense (Canadian Rule)
Offence: A crime or illegal act. (Canadian spelling uses 'c').

Offense: (American spelling – avoid unless referring to sports).

6. Ensure vs. Insure
Ensure: To make certain something happens. ("Ensure the door is locked.")
Insure: To protect financially. ("You must insure your vehicle.")

7. Stationary vs. Stationery
Stationary: Not moving. ("The patrol car was stationary.")
Stationery: Paper/Office supplies. ("Submit the report on official stationery.")

8. Principal vs. Principle
Principal: The head of a school OR the main person/thing. ("The principal suspect.")
Principle: A fundamental truth or rule. ("He is a man of high moral principle.")

9. Cite vs. Site vs. Sight
Cite: To quote or summon legally. ("He was cited for trespassing.")
Site: A location. ("The crime site.")
Sight: The ability to see. ("The suspect was out of sight.")

10. Their vs. There vs. They're
Their: Possession. ("It is their car.")
There: Location. ("Stand over there.")
They're: They are. ("They're under arrest.")

2. Essential Police Jargon SSPO Vocabulary

These words frequently appear in the "Synonyms" portion of Section A. You must know the definition.

11. Acquittal: A court judgment that a person is not guilty of the crime with which they have been charged.

12. Affidavit: A written statement confirmed by oath or affirmation, for use as evidence in court.

13. Alias: A false name or identity used to conceal one's true name.

14. Alleged: Said, without proof, to have taken place or to have a specified illegal or undesirable quality.

15. Appellant: A person who applies to a higher court for a reversal of the decision of a lower court.

16. Apprehend: To arrest someone for a crime.

17. Arraign: To call or bring someone before a court to answer a criminal charge.

18. Belligerent: Hostile and aggressive.

19. Breathalyzer: A device used for estimating blood alcohol content (BAC) from a breath sample.

20. Circumstantial: Pointing indirectly toward someone's guilt but not conclusively proving it.

21. Coerce: To persuade an unwilling person to do something by using force or threats.

22. Collusion: Secret or illegal cooperation or conspiracy, especially in order to cheat or deceive others.

23. Contraband: Goods that have been imported or exported illegally.

24. Corroborate: To confirm or give support to (a statement, theory, or finding).

25. Culpable: Deserving blame.

26. Defendant: An individual, company, or institution sued or accused in a court of law.

27. Detain: To keep (someone) in official custody, typically for questioning.

28. Deterrent: A thing that discourages or is intended to discourage someone from doing something.

29. Embezzle: To steal or misappropriate (money placed in one's trust or belonging to the organization for which one works).

30. Exonerate: To absolve (someone) from blame for a fault or wrongdoing.

31. Indictable: (In Canada) A serious crime bearing a heavier penalty (similar to a felony in the US).

32. Injunction: An authoritative warning or order.

33. Jurisdiction: The official power to make legal decisions and judgments.

34. Larceny: Theft of personal property.

35. Liability: The state of being responsible for something, especially by law.

36. Lieutenant: A rank of officer in the police force, above Sergeant.

37. Malice: The intention or desire to do evil; ill will.

38. Mandatory: Required by law or rules; compulsory.

39. Mitigate: To make less severe, serious, or painful.

40. Negligence: Failure to take proper care in doing something.

41. Occurrence: An incident or event.

42. Perjury: The offense of willfully telling an untruth in a court after having taken an oath or affirmation.

43. Perpetrator: A person who carries out a harmful, illegal, or immoral act.

44. Plaintiff: A person who brings a case against another in a court of law.

45. Recidivism: The tendency of a convicted criminal to reoffend.

46. Restitution: The restoration of something lost or stolen to its proper owner; recompense for injury or loss.

47. Sergeant: A rank of officer in the police force, above Constable and below Lieutenant.

48. Statute: A written law passed by a legislative body.

49. Subpoena: A writ ordering a person to attend a court.

50. Surveillance: Close observation, especially of a suspected spy or criminal.

3. The "Double-Letter" Trap List

These words are the most commonly misspelled on the SSPO because candidates forget which letters to double. Memorize these specific trouble spots.

51. **Accommodation:** (Two Cs, Two Ms).
52. **Aggressive:** (Two Gs, Two Ss).
53. **Apprehend:** (Two Ps).
54. **Assessment:** (Four Ss total).
55. **Barricade:** (Two Rs).
56. **Battalion:** (Two Ts, one L).
57. **Commission:** (Two Ms, Two Ss).
58. **Committee:** (Two Ms, Two Ts, Two Es).
59. **Corroborate:** (Two Rs in the first part).
60. **Embarrass:** (Two Rs, Two Ss).
61. **Exaggerate:** (Two Gs).
62. **Harassment:** (One R, Two Ss). Major Trap!
63. **Illicit:** (Two Ls).
64. **Interrogate:** (Two Rs).
65. **Misdemeanour:** (One S - mis + demeanour).
66. **Necessary:** (One C, Two Ss).
67. **Occurrence:** (Two Cs, Two Rs).
68. **Omission:** (One M, Two Ss).
69. **Possession:** (Four Ss total).
70. **Professional:** (One F, Two Ss).
71. **Reconnaissance:** (Two Ns, Two Ss).
72. **Sheriff:** (One R, Two Fs).
73. **Superintendent:** (No double letters! But often misspelled).
74. **Trespass:** (One S at start, Two Ss at end).
75. **Warrant:** (Two Rs).

PART 3 - GRAMMAR AND PUNCTUATION

ANSWER SHEET

	A	B	C	D
1	○	○	○	○
2	○	○	○	○
3	○	○	○	○
4	○	○	○	○
5	○	○	○	○
6	○	○	○	○
7	○	○	○	○
8	○	○	○	○
9	○	○	○	○
10	○	○	○	○

1. Which sentence is grammatically correct?

A. The officer apprehended the suspect, he was hiding behind the dumpster.

B. Hiding behind the dumpster, the officer apprehended the suspect.

C. The officer apprehended the suspect who was hiding behind the dumpster.

D. The officer apprehended the suspect, being that he was hiding behind the dumpster.

2. Select the sentence that is NOT a run-on sentence.

A. The witness provided a statement she was very cooperative.

B. The witness provided a statement; she was very cooperative.

C. The witness provided a statement, she was very cooperative.

D. The witness provided a statement being very cooperative.

3. Choose the sentence with the correct modifier placement.

A. Rushing to the scene, the siren wailed loudly.
B. The siren wailed loudly while rushing to the scene.
C. Rushing to the scene, the officer activated the siren.
D. The officer activated the siren, rushing to the scene.

4. The team of investigators _____ arriving tomorrow.

A. is

B. are

C. were

D. be

5. The suspect, along with his two accomplices, _____ arrested.

    A. were

    B. was

    C. are

    D. have been

6. Between you and _____, the case seems weak.

    A. I

    B. me

    C. myself

    D. mine

7. Who is the _____ ranking officer in this division?

    A. highest

    B. most high

    C. higher

    D. most highest

8. The _____ testimony contradicted the physical evidence.

    A. witness's

    B. witness'

    C. witnesses

    D. witnesss'

9. Which sentence is punctuated correctly?

    A. The suspect stopped his car, and opened the door.

    B. The suspect stopped his car and opened the door.

    C. The suspect stopped his car; and opened the door.

    D. The suspect, stopped his car and opened the door.

10. Identify the correct use of the semicolon.

A. The officer called for backup; however, no cars were available.

B. The officer called for backup, however; no cars were available.

C. The officer called for backup; however no cars were available.

D. The officer called for backup, however, no cars were available.

Answer Key and Explanation

1. C
Choice A is a comma splice (two independent clauses joined only by a comma). Choice B implies the officer was hiding (misplaced modifier). Choice D is wordy and awkward. Choice C correctly uses the relative clause "who was hiding" to modify the suspect.

2. B
Choices A and C are run-on sentences/comma splices. Choice D is a fragment/awkward phrasing. Choice B correctly joins two independent clauses with a semicolon.

3. C
The modifier "Rushing to the scene" must describe the subject immediately following it. The siren cannot "rush" (Sentence A). In Choice C, "the officer" is correctly modified by "Rushing to the scene."

4. A
"Team" is a collective noun acting as a single unit here, so it takes the singular verb "is."

5. B
Phrases like "along with," "as well as," or "together with" do not change the number of the subject. The subject is "The suspect" (singular), so the verb is "was."

6. B
"Between" is a preposition. Pronouns following prepositions must be in the object case ("me"), not the subject case ("I") or reflexive ("myself").

7. A
"Highest" is the correct superlative form. "Most high" is incorrect grammar.

8. A
"Witness" is singular. To make a singular noun possessive, add 's. (Witness's).

9. B

You do not use a comma before a conjunction (and) if the second part of the sentence is not an independent clause (it lacks a subject). "Opened the door" is just a second verb for the suspect, not a full sentence.

10. A

A semicolon joins two independent clauses. "However" is a transition word that usually takes a comma after it.

Section B: Police Problem Solving

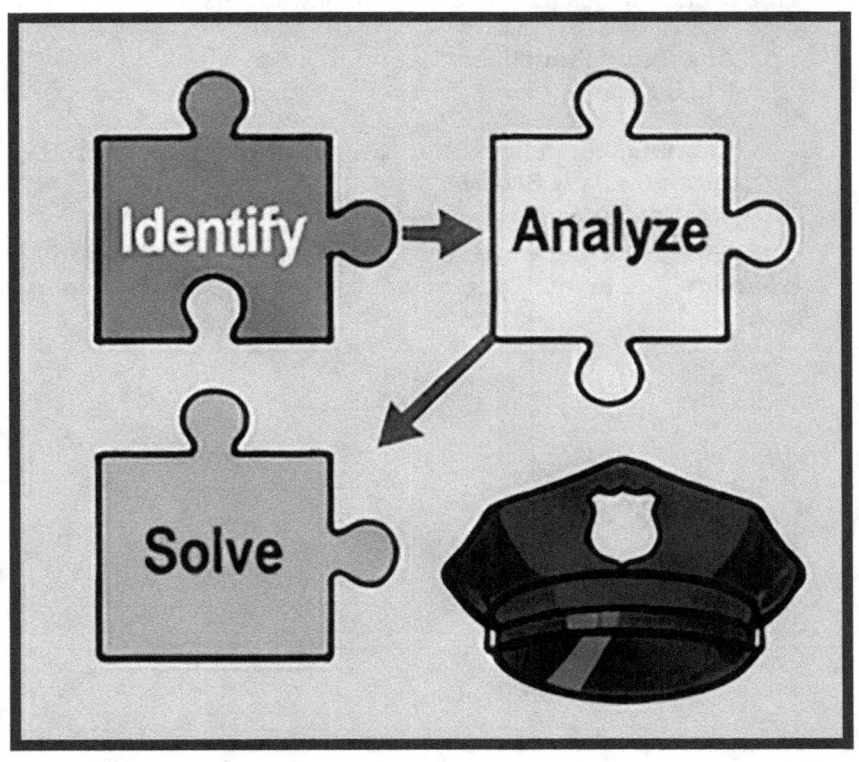

Part 1 - Rule Following

Rule Following & Integrity

This component of the personality assessment measures your willingness and natural inclination to adhere to established procedures, regulations, and the chain of command.

In policing, the ability to follow strict legal and procedural guidelines—even when no one is watching or when "bending the rules" might seem more efficient—is non-negotiable.

This section assesses whether you views rules as:

> **Absolute:** Guidelines that must always be followed (High Score).
>
> **Flexible:** Guidelines that can be adjusted based on the situation (Low Score).

You definitely want a high score in this area, as it indicates reliability, predictability, and low liability risk for the department.

Police Problem Solving

Answer Sheet

1. (A) (B) (C) (D)
2. (A) (B) (C) (D)
3. (A) (B) (C) (D)
4. (A) (B) (C) (D)
5. (A) (B) (C) (D)
6. (A) (B) (C) (D)

Rule Set 1: Property Offenses Classifications

Definitions:

Theft: Occurs when a person fraudulently and without color of right takes, or fraudulently converts to his/her own use, anything with intent to deprive the owner of it.

Robbery: Occurs when a person steals, and for the purpose of extorting whatever is stolen or to prevent or overcome resistance to the stealing, uses violence or threats of violence to a person or property.

Break and Enter: Occurs when a person enters a place with intent to commit an indictable offense therein. "Place" includes a dwelling-house, building, or structure.

Mischief: Occurs when a person willfully destroys or damages property, renders property dangerous, useless, inoperative, or ineffective, or obstructs, interrupts, or interferes with the lawful use, enjoyment, or operation of property.

1. Officer Chen responds to a call at a department store. A suspect was seen putting a smartwatch in his pocket and walking out the front door without paying. He did not speak to anyone. Based on the rules, how should this be classified?

    A) Robbery

    B) Break and Enter

    C) Theft D) Mischief

2. A suspect throws a brick through the window of a parked car, shattering the glass, but does not enter the car or take anything. Based on the rules, how is this classified?

    A) Attempted Theft

    B) Mischief

    C) Break and Enter

    D) Robbery

3. A suspect walks into a bank, hands the teller a note that says "Give me the money or I will hurt you," and flees with the cash. Based on the rules, this is:

    A) Theft
    B) Mischief
    C) Robbery
    D) Break and Enter

Rule Set 2: Traffic Enforcement & Towing Protocol

Rules:

    1. **Ticket (Offense Notice):** Issued for minor moving violations (speeding less than 30 km/h over limit, failing to stop) or minor document errors (expired license less than 1 month).

    2. **Summons:** Issued for major violations (speeding 30 km/h or more over limit, No Insurance) or repeat offenders.

    3. **Verbal Warning:** Issued only for equipment violations (broken taillight) where the driver agrees to fix it within 24 hours.

    4. **Vehicle Impoundment (Towing):** Mandatory if the driver has a suspended license OR is speeding 50 km/h or more over the limit.

    5. **License Seizure:** Mandatory if the driver has a suspended license.

4. Officer Patel stops a driver for speeding 60 km/h over the posted limit. The driver has a valid license. What is the required action?

    A) Issue a Ticket and release the driver.
    B) Issue a Summons and Impound the vehicle.
    C) Issue a Verbal Warning and Impound the vehicle.
    D) Issue a Ticket and Seize the license.

5. A driver is stopped for a broken taillight. The driver promises to fix it tomorrow. The driver has a valid license. What is the correct action?

    A) Issue a Ticket.

    B) Issue a Summons.

    C) Issue a Verbal Warning.

    D) Impound the vehicle.

6. A driver is stopped for speeding 40 km/h over the limit. What is the correct paperwork to issue?

    A) Verbal Warning

    B) Ticket (Offense Notice)

    C) Summons

    D) None of the above

Answer Key and Explanations

Rule Set 1: Property Offenses
1. C (Theft)

The suspect took the smartwatch fraudulently without color of right (didn't pay) and intended to deprive the owner. There was no violence (ruling out Robbery) and he walked through a door (ruling out Break and Enter).

Why the other choices are incorrect:

A (Robbery): Requires violence or threats. The suspect did not speak to or touch anyone.
B (Break and Enter): Requires entering a place to commit an offense. While he was in a store, entering a public store during hours is not usually "Breaking" unless specified, but primarily, the core offense here is the taking.
D (Mischief): The property was not damaged or rendered useless.

2. B (Mischief)

The suspect rendered the property (window) dangerous/useless and damaged it.

Choice A, Attempted Theft is incorrect. The scenario states he did not enter or try to take anything; he only broke the glass.
Choice D, Robbery is incorrect. No person was threatened.

3. C (Robbery)
The suspect stole cash AND used threats of violence ("I will hurt you") to overcome resistance.

Choice A, Theft, is incorrect. Theft does not include the element of threat/violence.
Choice B, Mischief, is incorrect. Property was not destroyed.

4. B (Issue a Summons and Impound the vehicle)
Speeding 60 km/h over fits Rule 2 (Summons for 30+ over) AND Rule 4 (Impound for 50+ over).
Choice A is incorrect. Ticket is only for speeding less than 30 km/h over.

5. C (Issue a Verbal Warning)
Broken taillight is an equipment violation. The driver agreed to fix it (Rule 3).
Choice A is incorrect. Tickets are for moving violations, not agreed-upon repairs.

6. C (Summons)
Speeding 40 km/h over is greater than the 30 km/h threshold for a Summons (Rule 2).

Choice B is incorrect. Tickets are for < 30 km/h over.

Map Reading & Directional Logic:

Mapping Self-Assessment

	A	B	C	D
1	○	○	○	○
2	○	○	○	○
3	○	○	○	○
4	○	○	○	○
5	○	○	○	○

Police Problem Solving

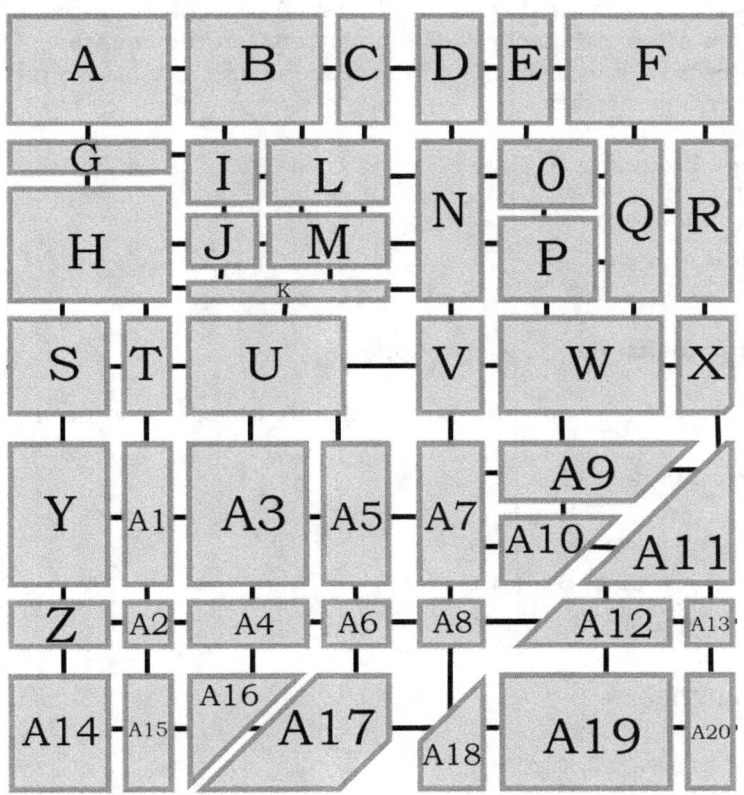

MAP KEY

Each square labeled A to Z and A1 to A20, represent the corner of an intersection. The lines between the squares represent a city block. The intersections and city blocks fall under 3 categories.

Large blocks: A, B,F, H, N, Q, R, U, W, Y, A3, A5, A7, A9, A11, A14, A17, A19

Small blocks: C, D, E, I. J, L,M, O, P, S, T, V, X, Z, A1, A4, A10, Z, A12, A15, A16, A18, A20

Mini blocks: G, K, A2, A6, A8, A13

The time it takes to travel from one city block to another is:

Large blocks

    In a car: 4 minutes
    On a bike: 6 minutes
    On foot: 10 minutes

Small Blocks

    In a car: 3 minutes
    On a bike: 5 minutes
    On foot: 8 minutes

Mini Blocks

    In a car: 2 minutes
    On a bike: 4 minutes
    On foot: 6 minutes

Police Problem Solving

1. What is the shortest time it would take a woman to go from block A to S driving a car?

    a. 11 minutes
    b. 7 and half minutes
    c. 8 minutes
    d. 10 minutes

2. What is the shortest time it would take a man to go from A to S if he drove the first two blocks, then rode a bike the rest of the way?

    a. 18 minutes
    b. 16 minutes
    c. 17 minutes
    d. 15 minutes

3. A student has to walk home from block U to R. What is the shortest time it would take him if he had to go through block Q?

    a. 38 minutes
    b. 32 minutes
    c. 37 minutes
    d. 29 minutes

4. A police patrol car in block Y has to respond to a call in Block G. How fast can they get there if they are forced by traffic to avoid Block S?

    a. 20 minutes
    b. 19 minutes
    c. 14 minutes
    d. 17 minutes

5. How fast would it take a man on bike to ride from block Z to block A7 if he had to spend two minutes and half along the way fixing his bike?

   a. 22. 5 minutes
   b. 22 minutes
   c. 24.5 minutes
   d. 24 minutes

POLICE PROBLEM SOLVING

ANSWER KEY

1. D
The shortest route would take a car through A – G – H - S, covering two large blocks and one mini block. This would take 10 minutes by car.

2. B
The shortest route from A to S is A – G – H – S, taking 6 minutes by car for the first 2 blocks and 10 minutes on a bike for the last large block. Total time is 16 minutes.

3. A
The shortest route from U to R passing through Q is U – V – W – Q – R. Time to walk these blocks is 38 minutes. (A)

4. C
The shortest route from block Y to G, avoiding S, is Y – A1 – T – H – G. Time by car is 14 minutes.

5. C
The fastest route is Z – A2 – A4 – A6 – A8 – A7. Time by bike is 22 minutes, plus 2.5 minutes to fix the bike, for a total of 24.5 minutes.

Ethical Judgment

1. The Coffee Shop Discount You are a rookie constable on patrol with a senior partner. You stop at a local coffee shop for a break. The manager, who knows your partner, refuses to take payment for the coffees, saying, "You guys do a great job keeping us safe; it's on the house." Your partner accepts the coffee and walks out.

What is the best way to handle this situation?

   A) Accept the coffee this time but insist on paying next time to be polite.

   B) Leave your money on the counter for your coffee and follow your partner out, then discuss it privately later.

   C) Refuse the coffee loudly so the other patrons know you are not corrupt.

   D) Accept the coffee; it is a small token of appreciation and refusing would be rude to a community member.

2. The Speeding Spouse While conducting traffic enforcement on a busy highway, you clock a vehicle traveling 35 km/h over the limit. You pull the vehicle over and realize the driver is the spouse of your Sergeant. The driver apologizes and mentions they are late picking up their child from school.

What is the best course of action?

   a) Issue a warning to avoid awkwardness at the station, as discretion is allowed.

   b) Call your Sergeant to ask how they would like you to handle the situation.

   c) Treat the driver exactly as you would any other citizen and issue the ticket based on the violation.

   d) Request another unit to attend the scene to issue the ticket to avoid a conflict of interest.

3. Social Media Comment You are off-duty and browsing a local community news page on social media. You see a heated comment thread regarding a recent arrest made by your police service. You know the details of the arrest and know that the public comments are factually incorrect and making the police look bad.

What is the best response?

> a) Post a comment from your personal account correcting the facts to protect the Service's reputation.
>
> b) Ignore the comments and do not engage, as you are off-duty.
>
> c) Post a comment anonymously stating that people should wait for the official report.
>
> d) Report the social media thread to your supervisor or the Public Information Officer for them to handle.

Answer Key & Detailed Explanations

1. The Coffee Shop Discount

- Correct Answer: B
- Difficulty: Medium
- Concept: Integrity / Gratuities

Why B is correct: This balances integrity with tactical awareness. You cannot accept the gratuity (violation of ethics/policy), so you pay. However, confronting a senior partner in front of the public (Option C) undermines public trust and chain of command. Discussing it privately addresses the ethical breach without causing a scene.

Why choice A is incorrect: "Paying next time" validates the current breach of ethics. Accepting gratuities creates a perception of indebtedness.
Why choice C is incorrect: While honest, "loudly refusing" is unprofessional and embarrasses the partner and the business owner.
Why choice D is incorrect: Police policy strictly forbids gratuities to prevent the perception of bias or "buying favor."

2. The Speeding Spouse

- Correct Answer: D
- Difficulty: Medium
- Concept: Conflict of Interest / Impartiality

This removes the conflict entirely. You cannot be objective (or perceived as objective) when dealing with your boss's spouse. Another officer can assess the situation impartially.

Why choice A is incorrect: Using discretion based on who the driver is (nepotism) is a serious ethical violation.
Why choice B is incorrect: Calling the Sergeant puts the Sergeant in an ethical bind and creates pressure.
Why choice C is incorrect: While technically "fair," the perception of bias remains. If the ticket is contested, your relationship makes the testimony vulnerable.

3. Social Media Comment

- Correct Answer: D
- Difficulty: Easy
- Concept: Professionalism / Media Relations

Police services have designated channels for releasing information. Reporting it allows the proper authorities to decide if a correction is strategically or legally appropriate.

Why choice A is incorrect: Officers generally cannot speak on behalf of the agency on personal accounts. It can jeopardize court cases.
Why choice B is incorrect: While better than posting, ignoring misinformation that damages public trust isn't proactive. Reporting it is the proactive step.
Why choice C is inocrrect: Posting anonymously is deceptive and lacks integrity.

Practice Test Questions 1

Ready to Test Your Skills? Below you will find a full-length practice test. Please note that these are not the exact questions from the official exam—those are kept secret and change every year. Instead, we have created questions that mirror the style and difficulty of the official test.

The Bottom Line: If you can answer these questions correctly, you have the knowledge needed to pass the real exam.

Practice Test Questions 1

Instructions:

Get in the Zone: Set aside uninterrupted time in a quiet room.

Focus: Read the instructions and every question carefully. Answer to the best of your ability.

Simulate: Use the provided bubble answer sheets to mimic the real test experience.

Review: Once finished, check your work against the Answer Key and read the explanations for any questions you missed.

Pro Tip: Do not attempt more than one practice test in a single day. Rest is just as important as practice. Wait 48 to 72 hours between tests for maximum retention.

Spelling Answer Sheet

	A	B	C	D
1	○	○	○	○
2	○	○	○	○
3	○	○	○	○
4	○	○	○	○
5	○	○	○	○
6	○	○	○	○
7	○	○	○	○
8	○	○	○	○
9	○	○	○	○
10	○	○	○	○
11	○	○	○	○
12	○	○	○	○
13	○	○	○	○
14	○	○	○	○
15	○	○	○	○

Vocabulary Answer Sheet

	A	B	C	D
1	○	○	○	○
2	○	○	○	○
3	○	○	○	○
4	○	○	○	○
5	○	○	○	○
6	○	○	○	○
7	○	○	○	○
8	○	○	○	○
9	○	○	○	○
10	○	○	○	○
11	○	○	○	○
12	○	○	○	○
13	○	○	○	○
14	○	○	○	○
15	○	○	○	○

Grammar & Punctuation Answer Sheet

	A	B	C	D
1	○	○	○	○
2	○	○	○	○
3	○	○	○	○
4	○	○	○	○
5	○	○	○	○
6	○	○	○	○
7	○	○	○	○
8	○	○	○	○
9	○	○	○	○
10	○	○	○	○
11	○	○	○	○
12	○	○	○	○
13	○	○	○	○
14	○	○	○	○
15	○	○	○	○

Rule Following Answer Sheet

	A	B	C	D
1	○	○	○	○
2	○	○	○	○
3	○	○	○	○
4	○	○	○	○
5	○	○	○	○
6	○	○	○	○
7	○	○	○	○
8	○	○	○	○
9	○	○	○	○
10	○	○	○	○
11	○	○	○	○
12	○	○	○	○
13	○	○	○	○
14	○	○	○	○
15	○	○	○	○

MAPPING ANSWER SHEET

	A	B	C	D
1	○	○	○	○
2	○	○	○	○
3	○	○	○	○
4	○	○	○	○
5	○	○	○	○
6	○	○	○	○
7	○	○	○	○
8	○	○	○	○
9	○	○	○	○
10	○	○	○	○
11	○	○	○	○
12	○	○	○	○
13	○	○	○	○
14	○	○	○	○
15	○	○	○	○

Ethics Answer Sheet

	A	B	C	D
1	○	○	○	○
2	○	○	○	○
3	○	○	○	○
4	○	○	○	○
5	○	○	○	○
6	○	○	○	○
7	○	○	○	○
8	○	○	○	○
9	○	○	○	○
10	○	○	○	○
11	○	○	○	○
12	○	○	○	○
13	○	○	○	○
14	○	○	○	○
15	○	○	○	○

Section A - Language
Spelling

Directions: Choose the correct spelling

1. A) Affidavit B) Affadavit C) Afidavit D) Affidavet

2. A) Defendant B) Defendent C) Deffendant D) Defendent

3. A) Acquited B) Aquitted C) Acquitted D) Akwitted

4. A) Neccessary B) Necassary C) Necessary D) Necesary

5. A) Embarrass B) Embarass C) Embaress D) Embarras

6. A) Possession B) Posesion C) Posession D) Possesion

7. A) Independant B) Independent C) Indipendant D) Indipendent

8. A) Recommend B) Reccomend C) Reccommend D) Recomend

9. A) Privilege B) Privalege C) Priviledge D) Privelige

10. A) Maintenence B) Maintainance C) Maintenance D) Maintnance

11. A) Vehicle B) Vehical C) Vehichle D) Vehecle

12. A) Aggressive B) Agressive C) Aggresive D) Agresive

13. A) Liaison B) Liason C) Liasson D) Layson

14. A) Bureaucracy B) Beurocracy C) Buraucracy D) Bureacracy

15. A) Forensics B) Forensicks C) Phorensics D) Forensiks

Vocabulary

Instructions
Read each sentence carefully. Select the word or phrase that best defines the **bolded** word as it is used in the context of the sentence.

1. The **perpetrator** fled the scene on foot wearing a red hoodie.

A) Victim B) Witness C) Offender D) Bystander

2. This highway is outside of the city police's **jurisdiction**.

A) Map B) Authority C) Interest D) Ability

3. The officer charged the landlord with **negligence** for failing to fix the fire alarm.

A) Carelessness B) Fraud C) Theft D) Malice

4. The suspect was booking flights under an **alias**.

A) Credit card B) False name C) Accomplice D) Plan

5. During the interview, the suspect showed genuine **remorse** for his actions.

A) Anger B) Pride C) Regret D) Fear

6. The judge's conditions **stipulate** that the accused cannot drink alcohol.

A) Suggest B) Specify C) Hope D) Deny

7. The detective did not find the witness's story **credible**.

A) Interesting B) Believable C) Useful D) Long

8. The employee was caught trying to **embezzle** funds from the company account.

A) Steal B) Deposit C) Borrow D) Donate

9. The protestors were arrested for trying to **incite** a riot.

A) Stop B) Film C) Provoke D) Watch

10. Police had to **detain** the individual for questioning regarding the robbery. A) Release B) Hold C) Charge D) Follow

11. The Crown Attorney decided to proceed with an **indictable** offense.

A) Minor B) Serious C) Traffic D) Civil

12. Wearing a seatbelt is **mandatory** in the province of Ontario.

A) Optional B) Required C) Suggested D) Dangerous

13. The suspect refused to **comply** with the officer's commands.

A) Listen B) Argue C) Obey D) Understand

14. The department decided to **rescind** the warrant after the error was discovered.

A) Cancel B) Execute C) Post D) Extend

15. The description of the vehicle was **ambiguous**, making it hard to locate.

A) Detailed B) Unclear C) Wrong D) Perfect

Grammar and Punctuation

1. Which of the following is a sentence fragment?

    A. Due to the heavy rainfall and poor visibility.

    B. The road was closed due to heavy rainfall.

    C. Visibility was poor because of the rain.

    D. Drivers were warned about the conditions.

2. Select the best way to combine these sentences: "The investigation was thorough. The evidence was conclusive."

    A. The investigation was thorough, the evidence was conclusive.

    B. The investigation was thorough; therefore, the evidence was conclusive.

    C. The investigation was thorough being that the evidence was conclusive.

    D. The investigation was thorough, however the evidence was conclusive.

3. Which sentence is the most concise and professional?

    A. It is the opinion of this officer that the suspect was intoxicated.

    B. I think the suspect might have been drunk.

    C. The suspect appeared intoxicated.

    D. The suspect, in my view, looked like he had too much to drink.

4. Please ensure that _____ aware of the new protocols.

    A) your
    B) you're
    C) yore
    D) ur

5. The department has _____ resources than it did last year.

    A) less
    B) fewer
    C) lesser
    D) least

6. If I _____ you, I would request backup.

    A) was
    B) am
    C) were
    D) be

7. The constable _____ the file on the desk.

    A) lay
    B) laid
    C) lied
    D) lain

8. Everyone must submit _____ badge for inspection.

    A) their
    B) there
    C) his or her
    D) they're

9. Choose the sentence with correct comma usage.

A) "Stop" shouted the officer "or I will use force."
B) "Stop," shouted the officer, "or I will use force."
C) "Stop", shouted the officer, "or I will use force."
D) "Stop," shouted the officer "or I will use force."

10. Which is the correct possessive form?

A) The mens' locker room
B) The men's locker room
C) The mens locker room
D) The mens's locker room

Identify the punctuation mistake in the underlined phrase.

11. Ted and Janice <u>who had been friends for years went on vacation together</u> every summer.

A) Ted and Janice, who had been friends for years, went on vacation together every summer.
B) Ted and Janice who had been friends for years, went on vacation together every summer.
C) Ted, and Janice who had been friends for years, went on vacation together every summer.
D) None of the choices are correct.

12. None of us want to go to the <u>party not even</u> if there will be live musiC)

A) None of us want to go to the party not even, if there will be live musiC)
B) None of us want to go to the party, not even if there will be live musiC)
C) None of us want to go to the party; not even if there will be live musiC)
D) None of the choice are correct.

13. <u>John, Maurice, and Thomas,</u> quit school two months before graduation.

    A) John, Maurice, and Thomas quit school two months before graduation.

    B) John, Maurice and Thomas quit school two months before graduation.

    C) John Maurice and Thomas, quit school two months before graduation.

    D) None of the choice are correct.

14. She is the <u>most cleverest</u> girl in the class.

    A) She is the most clever girl in the class.

    B) She is the cleverest girl in the class.

    C) She is the most cleverer girl in the class.

    D) None of the above.

15. He <u>lived</u> in California since 1995.

    A) He had lived in California since 1995.

    B) He has been living in California since 1995.

    C) He has living in California since 1995.

    D) None of the above.

Section B: Police Problem Solving

Rule Application

Instructions: For each set of questions, read the provided "Rules and Definitions" carefully. Answer the questions based ONLY on the information provided in the rules. Do not use outside knowledge of actual laws.

Rule Set 1: Property Offenses Classifications

Definitions:

> **Theft:** Occurs when a person fraudulently and without color of right takes, or fraudulently converts to his/her own use, anything with intent to deprive the owner of it.
>
> **Robbery:** Occurs when a person steals, and for the purpose of extorting whatever is stolen or to prevent or overcome resistance to the stealing, uses violence or threats of violence to a person or property.
>
> **Break and Enter:** Occurs when a person enters a place with intent to commit an indictable offense therein. "Place" includes a dwelling-house, building, or structure.
>
> **Mischief:** Occurs when a person willfully destroys or damages property, renders property dangerous, useless, inoperative, or ineffective, or obstructs, interrupts, or interferes with the lawful use, enjoyment, or operation of property.

1. A suspect forces a lock on a backyard shed, enters, and looks around for tools to steal but flees when a light turns on. He takes nothing. Based on the rules, this is:

  A) Attempted Theft
  B) Break and Enter
  C) Mischief
  D) Trespassing

2. A person enters an unlocked garage attached to a house intending to steal a bicycle. Based on the rules, this is:

  A) Theft
  B) Mischief
  C) Break and Enter
  D) Robbery

3. During a heated argument, a suspect grabs the victim's cell phone and smashes it on the ground, shattering it. He does not take the phone parts. Based on the rules, this is:

  A) Theft
  B) Robbery
  C) Break and Enter
  D) Mischief

Rule Set 2: Traffic Enforcement & Towing Protocol Rules:

  1. Ticket (Offense Notice): Issued for minor moving violations (speeding less than 30 km/h over limit, failing to stop) or minor document errors (expired license less than 1 month).

  2. Summons: Issued for major violations (speeding 30 km/h or more over limit, No Insurance) or repeat offenders.

3. **Verbal Warning:** Issued only for equipment violations (broken taillight) where the driver agrees to fix it within 24 hours.

4. **Vehicle Impoundment (Towing):** Mandatory if the driver has a suspended license OR is speeding 50 km/h or more over the limit.

5. **License Seizure:** Mandatory if the driver has a suspended license.

4. Officer Lee stops a driver for running a stop sign (a minor moving violation). The driver's license expired 2 weeks ago. What should Officer Lee issue?

    A) Verbal Warning for both.

    B) Summons for the license; Ticket for the stop sign.

    C) Ticket for the stop sign; Ticket for the expired license.

    D) Summons for both.

5. A driver is stopped. A check reveals their license is suspended. They were not speeding. What are the mandatory actions?

    A) Issue Summons and release the vehicle.

    B) Seize License and Impound Vehicle.

    C) Issue Ticket and Seize License.

    D) Issue Verbal Warning and Impound Vehicle.

6. A driver is stopped for speeding 15 km/h over the limit. What is the correct action?

    A) Verbal Warning

    B) Summons

    C) Impound Vehicle

    D) Ticket (Offense Notice)

7. A driver is stopped for No Insurance. Based on the rules, what paperwork is issued?

    A) Ticket

    B) Verbal Warning

    C) Summons

    D) Notification of Impound

Rule Set 3: Use of Force Continuum

Rules:

> **Level 1 (Officer Presence):** Use when subject is cooperative.
>
> **Level 2 (Verbal Communication):** Use when subject is passively resistant (refusing to move, ignoring commands) but not physical.
>
> **Level 3 (Soft Physical Control):** (Holds, joint locks) Use when subject is actively resistant (pulling away, running away) but not attacking.
>
> **Level 4 (Hard Physical Control):** (Strikes, baton) Use when subject is assaultive (kicking, punching, biting) causing risk of bodily harm.
>
> **Level 5 (Lethal Force):** Use when subject poses a threat of death or grievous bodily harm to officer or public.

8. A suspect is sitting on the ground refusing to stand up when ordered. He is not moving his arms or legs, just going limp. What is the appropriate level of force?

    A) Level 1

    B) Level 2

    C) Level 3

    D) Level 4

9. An officer arrives at a scene and the suspect immediately puts their hands in the air and says "I give up." What level of force is appropriate?

    A) Level 1
    B) Level 2
    C) Level 3
    D) Level 4

10. When an officer attempts to handcuff a suspect, the suspect yanks their arm away and tries to run. The suspect does not try to hit the officer. What is the maximum appropriate level?

    A) Level 2
    B) Level 3
    C) Level 4
    D) Level 5

11. A suspect pulls a knife and charges at a bystander. What level is authorized?

    A) Level 2
    B) Level 3
    C) Level 4
    D) Level 5

12. A suspect punches an officer in the face. What level is authorized?

    A) Level 2
    B) Level 3
    C) Level 4
    D) Level 5

Rule Set 4: Public Park Bylaws

Rules:

Zone A (Playground): Open 9:00 AM to Sundown. No dogs allowed. No alcohol.

Zone B (Picnic Area): Open 8:00 AM to 11:00 PM. Dogs allowed on leash. Alcohol allowed with permit.

Zone C (Trails): Open Sunrise to Sunset. Dogs allowed off-leash. No alcohol. No bicycles.

Enforcement:

Violation of Hours: $100 Fine.

Violation of Alcohol Policy: $200 Fine.

Violation of Dog Policy: $50 Fine.

13. It is 2:00 PM. Officer Gomez sees a man walking a dog on a leash in Zone A. What is the correct enforcement action?

A) $100 Fine

B) $200 Fine

C) $50 Fine

D) No violation

14. A group is having a picnic in Zone B at 10:00 PM. They are drinking beer and have a valid permit. What is the enforcement action?

A) $100 Fine (Hours)

B) $200 Fine (Alcohol)

C) Evict them from the park.

D) No violation.

15. A cyclist is riding through Zone C at noon. What is the violation?

    A) Violation of Dog Policy.

    B) Violation of Alcohol Policy.

    C) Violation of Hours.

    D) The rules do not specify a fine for bicycles, but it is prohibited.

Mapping

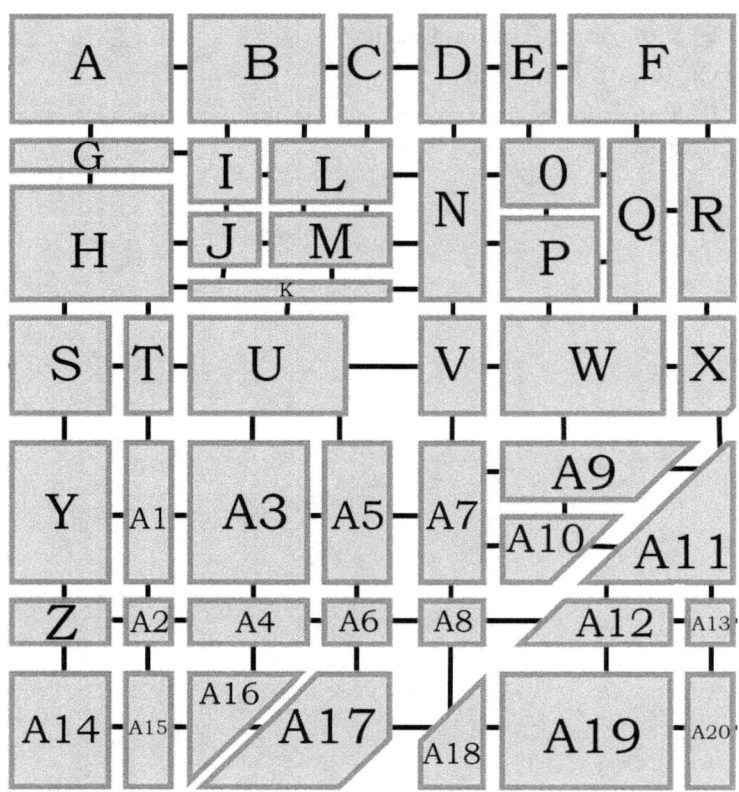

Map Key

Each Square labeled A to Z and A1 to A20 represent the corner of an intersection. The lines between the squares represent a city block. The intersections and city blocks fall into 3 categories.

Large blocks: A, B, F, H, N, Q, R, U, W, Y, A3, A5, A7, A9, A11, A14, A17, A19

Small blocks: C, D, E, I. J, L, M, O, P, S, T, V, X, Z, A1, A4, A10, Z, A12, A15, A16, A18, A20

Mini blocks: G, K, A2, A6, A8, A13

The time it to travel between city block is:

Large blocks

In a car: 4 minutes
On a bike: 6 minutes
On foot: 10 minutes

Small Blocks

In a car: 3 minutes
On a bike: 5 minutes
On foot: 8 minutes

Mini Blocks

In a car: 2 minutes
On a bike: 4 minutes
On foot: 6 minutes

1. A car travels from block X to A6. What is the shortest possible time it would spend if it had to spend 2 minutes to buy gas?

    A) 15 minutes
    B) 12 minutes
    C) 17 minutes
    D) 14 minutes

2. How fast can you walk from block B to V without passing through blocks L and N?

   A) 52 minutes
   B) 42 minutes
   C) 45 minutes
   D) 38 minutes

3. A pizza delivery boy on bike in block A9 has to make a delivery in A20. What is the shortest time it would take him to get if he rides his bike the first 2 blocks and walks the rest of the way?

   A) 18 minutes
   B) 20 minutes
   C) 17 minutes
   D) 22 minutes

4. A car moves from block Y to block A17. Along the way it goes through block A2 and A5. What is the shortest time it could have taken if it is not allowed to go through the same block twice?

   A) 19 minutes
   B) 29 minutes
   C) 20 minutes
   D) 22 minutes

5. What is the shortest time it would take to bike from block H to block A4 if you must pass through block Y?

   A) 30 minutes
   B) 26 minutes
   C) 18 minutes
   D) 28 minutes

6. How fast can it take a police car to travel from block Z to V if it has to spend 15 seconds extra at each intersection it drives pass?

   A) 15 minutes 45 seconds
   B) 16 minutes 45 seconds
   C) 17 minutes
   D) 17 minutes 45 seconds

7. Which of the following would be the shortest?

Driving from block Z to A12
Walking from block A to D
Driving from A to C and then walking to D
Riding a bike from block T to A14

   A) driving from block z to a12
   B) walking from block a to d
   C) driving from a to c and then walking to d
   D) riding a bike from block t to a14

8. Which of these would take the most time?

Walking from A3 to K
Riding a bike from A3 to A10
Driving a car from A3 to S
Riding a bike from A3 to y, then driving a car to H

   A) walking from a3 to k
   B) riding a bike from a3 to a10
   C) driving a car from a3 to s
   D) riding a bike from a3 to y, then driving a car to h

9. If you had to spend 15 extra seconds at each intersection, how long would it take from block F to block V by bike, using the shortest route?

    A) 15 minutes
    B) 12 minutes
    C) 14 minutes
    D)   17 minutes

10. A driver needs to go from block F to V. How many possible route combinations can he use if he must pass through only 4 blocks between F and V?

    A) 5 routes
    B) 4 routes
    C) 3 routes
    D) 6 routes

11. A driver needs to drive from block F to V. What is the fastest time he can use if he must pass through only 4 blocks between F and V?

    A) 15 minutes
    B) 16 minutes
    C) 17 minutes
    D) 19 minutes

12. How fast would a bike rider move from block H to X?

    A) 24 minutes
    B) 27 minutes
    C) 25 minutes
    D) 26 minutes

13. How long would it take a man to move from block H to X if he drove a car the first 3 blocks and then rode a bike the rest of the way, using the fastest route?

    A) 18 minutes
    B) 21 minutes
    C) 22 minutes
    D) 20 minutes

14. How long would it take to move from block D to A6, by car for the first block, by bike for the next 2 blocks and then on foot the rest of the way, using the fastest route?

    A) 30 minutes
    B) 25 minutes
    C) 32 minutes
    D) 28 minutes

15. How fast does it take by bike from block G to P with a one minute stop at each intersection?

    A) 22 minutes
    B) 19 minutes
    C) 23 minutes
    D) 25 minutes

Ethical Judgment

1. The Forgotten Evidence (Level 3 - High Difficulty)
You are preparing for court and realize you forgot to log a minor piece of physical evidence in your notebook during the initial arrest six months ago. The evidence supports the charge but isn't the only proof. If you admit the mistake now, the defense might use it to discredit your organizational skills, potentially weakening the case.

What is the best course of action?

> A) Add the entry to your notebook now and backdate it, as it is what actually happened.
>
> B) Do not mention the evidence in court and rely on the other proof to secure the conviction.
>
> C) Disclose the omission to the Crown Attorney (Prosecutor) immediately and document the error in a current report.
>
> D) Testify about the evidence as if it were properly logged, assuming no one will check the specific dates in the notebook.

2. The Sick Day You wake up feeling perfectly fine, but you have a significant amount of accumulated sick leave. You really want to attend a concert tonight that you previously couldn't get time off for. You consider calling in sick.

What is the best way to view this situation?

> A) Call in sick; the time is yours to use and mental health days are important.
>
> B) Go to work as scheduled; using sick time when not sick is fraudulent and burdens your colleagues.
>
> C) Call in sick but stay home to ensure you don't get caught at the concert.
>
> D) Ask a colleague to switch shifts with you at the last minute; if they can't, call in sick.

3. The Excessive Force Witness During a chaotic arrest involving a resisting suspect, you witness your partner strike the suspect after the suspect has already been handcuffed and is under control. The suspect sustains a minor injury.

What is the best course of action?

A) Pull your partner aside immediately and tell them to calm down, but do not report it unless the suspect complains.

B) Write your report omitting the strike to protect your partner, as the suspect was resisting earlier.

C) Intervene immediately to ensure the suspect's safety, and report the incident to your supervisor as soon as the situation is secure.

D) Advise the suspect to file a complaint against your partner so the investigation is handled by third parties.

4. The Background Check (Level 1 - Easy) Your sister is starting a new business partnership with a man she met recently. She is worried about his past and asks you to run his name through the police database (CPIC) just to see if he has a criminal record. She promises to keep it a secret.

What is the best course of action?

A) Run the check this one time to ensure your sister's safety, but tell her not to tell anyone.

B) Refuse the request and explain that accessing the database for personal reasons is a criminal offense and a breach of policy.

C) Ask a colleague to run the check so your login ID isn't associated with the search.

D) Tell your sister you can't do it, but suggest she ask a private investigator who might have access.

5. The Impaired Colleague (Level 3 - High Difficulty) You are off-duty at a bar and see a fellow officer, who is also off-duty, drinking heavily. You watch them stumble out to the parking lot and get into the driver's seat of their personal vehicle. They start the engine.

What is the best course of action?

A) Call the on-duty patrol supervisor immediately to intercept the vehicle.

B) Run out and attempt to stop them from driving; if they refuse, call 911 immediately.

C) Take a photo of the license plate and report it to Professional Standards the next morning.

D) Do nothing; they are off-duty and it is not your place to police other officers in their private time.

6. The Inappropriate Joke You are in the break room with several other officers. A senior officer tells a joke that targets a specific ethnic group. Most of the officers laugh, but you find the joke offensive and contrary to the Service's values of diversity and inclusion.

What is the best response?

A) Laugh along awkwardly to fit in with the team and avoid being ostracized.

B) Stay silent and leave the room immediately, then complain to your friends later.

C) Confront the officer immediately in front of everyone, stating the joke is racist and unacceptable.

D) Do not laugh; speak to the officer privately afterwards to explain why the comment was inappropriate, or report it to a supervisor if the behavior is part of a pattern.

7. The Domestic Call Bias You respond to a domestic disturbance. One of the parties involved is a well-known local politician who has been very supportive of the police budget. The politician implies that if you arrest them, it will "hurt the department" in the long run. There are clear grounds for assault charges against the politician.

What is the best course of action?

> A) Arrest the politician based on the evidence of the assault; the law applies to everyone equally.
>
> B) Issue a warning and separate the parties for the night to avoid political fallout.
>
> C) Call the Chief of Police directly to ask for permission to make the arrest.
>
> D) Arrest the other party (the victim) instead, as they are less likely to cause trouble for the department.

8. The Found Wallet While patrolling a park, you find a wallet containing $200 cash but no ID. There are no witnesses around. You are struggling financially and the money would help pay a bill.

What is the best course of action?

> A) Take the cash as a "perk" of the job since there is no way to return it.
>
> B) Leave the wallet where it is; someone else will find it.
>
> C) Log the wallet and cash into the property room as "found property" according to procedure.
>
> D) Donate the money to a local charity so it goes to a good cause.

9. The Mental Health Crisis (Level 3 - High Difficulty)
You respond to a call of a man with a knife in a park. Upon arrival, you see the man holding a small knife, pacing in a circle, shouting at people who are not there. He is about 20 feet away from you and 30 feet from the nearest civilian. He does not appear aggressive towards you, but is clearly in distress.

What is the best course of action?

A) Draw your firearm and scream at him to drop the knife immediately; if he doesn't, use force to neutralize the threat. B) Draw your Taser (CEW) and immediately deploy it to secure him before he can hurt anyone.

C) Maintain distance and cover, clear civilians from the area, and attempt to de-escalate verbally while waiting for backup/specialized units. D) Rush him while he is distracted to tackle him and disarm him physically.

10. The Courtroom Error You are testifying in a trial regarding a drug bust you conducted a year ago. During cross-examination by the defense lawyer, you confidently state that you found the drugs in the "left pocket" of the suspect's jacket. During the break, you check your notes and realize you actually wrote "right pocket."

What is the best course of action?

A) Stick to your testimony; changing it now will look like you are lying or incompetent, and the location of the pocket is a minor detail.

B) Ask to speak to the Judge privately to explain the mistake.

C) When court resumes, ask to clarify your previous statement, admit the error, and correct the record based on your notes.

D) Say nothing, but if asked again, say you "don't recall" to avoid contradicting yourself.

11. The Supervisor's Request = Your Sergeant hands you a report for an arrest that happened while you were on lunch break. He says, "I need a second signature on this to process the prisoner faster. Just sign it as the witnessing officer; I was there, it's all good." You did not witness the arrest.

What is the best course of action?

A) Sign the report; you trust your Sergeant and efficiency is important for the team.

B) Refuse to sign and report the Sergeant to the Superintendent immediately for attempted fraud.

C) Refuse to sign the report, explaining that you cannot attest to events you did not witness, but offer to help process the prisoner in other ways.

D) Sign the report but add a small note next to your signature saying "did not witness."

12. The Racial Profiling Suspicions You are riding with a new partner. He suggests pulling over a luxury vehicle. When you ask for the cause, he says, "Look at the driver. A guy like that can't afford a car like that legally. Probably a drug dealer." The driver is a person of color. There is no traffic violation.

What is the best response?

A) Agree to the stop; your partner might have intuition you don't have.

B) Firmly refuse to initiate the stop, explaining that race and economic status are not reasonable grounds for detention, and it violates human rights.

C) Conduct the stop but be extra polite to the driver to make up for the lack of grounds.

D) Stay silent and let him drive, but note the time in your notebook in case there is a complaint later.

13. The Spilled Evidence You are seizing a bag of white powder (suspected cocaine) during a search. As you are placing it into an evidence bag, the baggie rips and some powder falls onto the muddy ground, mixing with the dirt.

What is the best course of action?

A) Scrape up the mud and powder mixture, put it in the bag, and don't mention the spill so the weight matches.

B) Dispose of the spilled portion and only log the powder that remained clean, estimating the weight of the lost amount. C) Photograph the spill, collect the remaining clean powder, collect the contaminated sample separately, and document exactly what happened in your report.

D) Replace the spilled powder with baking soda from the kitchen so the evidence weight is correct for court.

14. The Counter-Protest You are assigned to crowd control. A peaceful protest is met by a smaller, angry group of counter-protesters. The counter-protesters are shouting insults. The main group is starting to shout back. Tension is rising. What is the best course of action?

A) Order the counter-protesters to leave immediately as they are the ones causing the problem.

B) Position yourself and your team between the two groups to create a physical barrier, protecting the right of both groups to speak while preventing physical contact.

C) Arrest the loudest people on both sides to calm the crowd. D) Do nothing until the first punch is thrown, then react with force.

15. The Off-Duty Robbery (Level 3 - High Difficulty) You are off-duty, shopping in a convenience store with your family. A man enters with a knife and demands cash from the clerk. He is not physically attacking anyone yet. You are armed with your personal off-duty firearm (in jurisdictions where this applies) or have access to a weapon. What is the best course of action?

A) Draw your weapon and challenge the suspect immediately to stop the robbery.

B) tackle the suspect from behind while he is focused on the clerk.

C) Be a "good witness"—observe, get a good description, ensure your family is safe, and call 911 immediately. Only intervene physically if the suspect starts hurting someone. D) Yell "Police!" to scare him off.

Answer Key and Explanation

1. A) Affidavit

Tip: Double F, but only one 'd'.

2. A) Defendant

Tip: Think of an Ant defending its hill. The suffix is -ant.

3. C) Acquitted

Tip: Remember the 'cq' blend, and because the stress is on 'quit', you double the 't'.

4. C) Necessary

Tip: Think of a shirt: One Collar (c), Two Sleeves (ss).

5. A) Embarrass

Tip: Like accommodate, it's large. Double R, Double S.

6. A) Possession

Tip: It possesses a lot of S's. Double S twice (ss... ss).

7. B) Independent

Tip: There are 'dent's on both ends. In - depen - dent. No 'ants' allowed.

8. A) Recommend

Tip: One C, Two Ms. Think "Re-Commend".

9. A) Privilege

Tip: Two 'i's, two 'e's. No 'd' in the middle! It is not "ledge".

10. C) Maintenance

Tip: The root word "Maintain" changes to "Mainten" when it becomes a noun. It loses the 'ai'.

11. A) Vehicle

Tip: Don't forget the silent 'h' inside. Ve-hic-le.

12. A) Aggressive

Tip: Aggressive people want more. Double G, Double S.

13. A) Liaison

Tip: A very tricky French loan word. Remember the vowel string: l-i-a-i-s-o-n.

14. A) Bureaucracy

Tip: Start with Bureau (like a dresser). Then add -cracy.

15. A) Forensics

Tip: Phonetic spelling, but remember it uses 's', not 'cks' at the end.

Vocabulary

1. C) Offender.
A perpetrator is a person who carries out a harmful, illegal, or immoral act.

2. B) Authority.
Jurisdiction is the official power to make legal decisions and judgments in a specific area.

3. A) Carelessness.
Negligence is failure to take proper care in doing something.

4. B) False name.
An alias is a false identity.

5. C) Regret.
Remorse is deep regret or guilt for a wrong committed.

6. B) Specify.
Stipulate means to demand or specify a requirement, typically as part of a bargain or agreement.

7. B) Believable.
Credible means able to be believed; convincing.

8. A) Steal.
Embezzle means to steal or misappropriate (money placed in one's trust).

9. C) Provoke.
Incite means to encourage or stir up violent or unlawful behavior.

10. B) Hold.
Detain means to keep (someone) in official custody, typically for questioning.

11. B) Serious.
In Canada, an indictable offense is a serious crime (similar to a felony in the US).

12. B) Required.
Mandatory means required by law or rules; compulsory.

13. C) Obey.
Comply means to act in accordance with a wish or command.

14. A) Cancel.
Rescind means to revoke, cancel, or repeal (a law, order, or agreement).

15. B) Unclear. |
Ambiguous means open to more than one interpretation; having a double meaning. 26. B) Stray. Deviate means to depart from an established course.

Grammar and Punctuation

1. A
A lacks a main verb and a complete thought. It is a dependent phrase functioning as a fragment.

2. B
"Therefore" is a conjunctive adverb that logically connects the two ideas. It requires a semicolon before and a comma after when connecting independent clauses.

3. C
Police reports require concise, objective, and factual language. A is too wordy ("It is the opinion..."). B and D use subjective or colloquial language ("I think," "drunk").

4. B
You need the contraction for "you are." "Your" is possessive.

5. B
Use "fewer" for items that can be counted (resources, cars, people). Use "less" for bulk quantities or abstract concepts (less water, less courage).

6. C
This is the subjunctive mood, used for hypothetical situations. "If I were..." is the correct form.

7. B
"Laid" means to put something down (past tense of lay). "Lay" (past tense of lie) means to recline. The constable put the file down.

8. C
"Everyone" is an indefinite singular pronoun. Traditionally, it requires a singular possessive ("his or her"). "Their" is becoming common but "his or her" is safer for formal grammar tests.

9. B
Commas are placed inside the quotation marks. The attribution (shouted the officer) is set off by commas on both sides.

10. B
"Men" is already plural. To make a plural noun that does not end in 's' possessive, add 's.

11. A
Use a comma to separate phrases.

12. B
Use a comma separates independent clauses. None of us wants to go to the party, not even if there will be live music.

13. B
Don't use a comma before 'and' in a list.

14. B
Cleverest is the proper form to express 'most cleverer.'

15. B
Past perfect continuous, has been living, is proper because the time element, since 1995, and he is still living there now.

Section B: Police Problem Solving

Rule Application

1. B (Break and Enter)
The suspect entered a "place" (shed/structure) with the intent to commit an indictable offense (stealing tools). The offense does not need to be completed; the entry with intent is sufficient.

Choice A, Attempted Theft, is incorrect. While true, B&E is the more specific classification for the act of entering the structure. In police testing, B&E hierarchy usually supersedes simple attempt theft.
Choice C, Mischief, is incorrect. He forced the lock, which is damage, but the intent to steal makes it B&E.

2. C (Break and Enter)
A garage is a structure/place. He entered with intent to steal. It does not matter if it was unlocked.

Choice A, Theft is incorrect. He hasn't taken the bike yet.
Choice D, Robbery is incorrect. No violence against a person.

3. D (Mischief)
He destroyed the property (phone). He did not take it for his own use (ruling out Theft).

Choice B, Robbery, is incorrect. Robbery requires stealing (taking). He destroyed it on the spot.

4. C (Ticket for the stop sign; Ticket for the expired license)
Stop sign is a minor moving violation (Rule 1). Expired license < 1 month (2 weeks) is a minor document error (Rule 1). Both get Tickets.

Choices B & D are incorrect. Summons are for major violations.

5. B (Seize License and Impound Vehicle)
Rule 5 requires License Seizure for suspended drivers. Rule 4 requires Vehicle Impoundment for suspended drivers.

Choice C is incorrect. A Ticket does not address the suspended license seizure requirement.

6. D (Ticket)
Speeding 15 km/h over is less than 30 km/h (Rule 1).

Choice A is incorrect. Verbal warnings are for equipment, not moving violations.

7. C (Summons)
Rule 2 explicitly lists "No Insurance" as a Summons offense.

Choice A is incorrect. Tickets are for minor offenses. No Insurance is a major offense.

8. B (Level 2)
The subject is "passively resistant" (refusing to move, but not pulling away). Rule for passive resistance is Level 2 (Verbal).

Choice C, Level 3, is incorrect. Requires active resistance (pulling away).

9. A (Level 1)
The subject is cooperative.

Choice B, Verbal commands, is incorrect. This is are for resistance.

10. B (Level 3)
The subject is "pulling away" and "running." This matches the definition of "Actively Resistant," which authorizes Soft Physical Control (Level 3).

Choice C, Level 4, is incorrect. The subject is not attacking/assaultive.

11. D (Level 5)
Charging a bystander with a knife poses a "threat of death or grievous bodily harm."

Choice C, Level 4, is incorrect. Hard physical is for assault (kicking/punching) but a knife elevates the threat to lethal.

12. C (Level 4)
Punching an officer is "assaultive," which authorizes Hard Physical Control.

Choice B, is incorrect. Soft physical is for pulling away, not hitting.

13. C ($50 Fine)
Zone A prohibits dogs (No dogs allowed). The presence of the dog is the violation. Violation of Dog Policy = $50.

Choice D is incorrect. Even though on a leash, they are in a "No dogs" zone.

14. D (No violation)
Time: 10:00 PM is within open hours (8am-11pm).
Activity: Drinking with permit is allowed in Zone B.

Choices A & B are incorrect. No rules were broken.

15. D (The rules do not specify a fine for bicycles, but it is prohibited)
This is a logic trap. Zone C says "No bicycles." However, the "Enforcement" list only gives fines for Hours, Alcohol, and Dogs. You cannot invent a fine amount if it isn't listed.

Choices A, B, C: It is none of these specific violations.

Mapping

1. D
The fastest route is through blocks X – A11 – A12 – A8 – A6. Time by car is 12 plus 2 minutes to buy gas is 14 minutes.

2. B
The fastest route is B – I – J – K – U – V. Time on foot is 42 minutes.

3. A
The Fastest route is A9 – A11 – A13 – A20. By bike the first two blocks would take 12 minutes. To walk the last block would take 6 minutes. Total time is 18 minutes.

4. D
Fastest route is Y – Z – A2 – A1 – A3 – A5 – A6 – A7. By car it would take 22 minutes.

5. B
Fastest route is H – S – Y – Z – A2 – A4. Time by bike is 26 minutes.

6. B
The fastest route from Z to V is Z – A2- A4 – A6 – A8 – A7 – V. Total drive time is 16 minutes. From Z would go through 5 intersections. 15 seconds at each intersection is 45 seconds. Total time is 16 minutes, 45 seconds.

7. A
Driving from block Z to A12 would take 12 minutes.
Walking from block A to D would take 28 minutes
Driving from A to C and then walking to D would take 16 minutes
Riding a bike from block T to A14 would take 19 minutes.
The shortest trip would be driving from block Z to A12.

8. A
Walking from A3 to K would take 20 minutes
Riding a bike from A3 to A10 would take 11 minutes
Driving a car from A3 to S would take 11 minutes

Riding a bike from A3 to y, then driving a car to H would take 17 minutes
The most time would be to walk from A3 to K (A)

9. C
The shortest route from F to V is F – Q – W – V. The time on bike is 14 minutes.

10. A
Possible routes between F and V that goes through just 4 blocks are?
F – Q – R – X – W – V
F – E – O – P - W – V
F - E - O - Q - W – V
F - Q - W - P -N – V
F - Q - O - P - W – V
There are 5 possible routes.

11. C
There are 5 possible routes from block F to V that goes through just 4 blocks. 4 of the 5 routes take the least time of 17 minutes each.

12. B
The fastest route from H to X is H – K – N – V – W – X. On a bike that would take 27 minutes.

13. D
The fastest route from H to X is H – K – N – V – W – X. On foot for the first 3 blocks, it would take 9 minutes plus 11 minutes by bike to X. Total time is 20 minutes.

14. A
The fastest route is D – N – V – A7 – A8 - A6. To drive the first block is 3 minutes, then by bike the next 2 blocks is 11 minutes, and the on foot the last 2 blocks is 16 minutes. Total time is 30 minutes.

15. C
The fastest route is G – I – L – N – P. By bike it would take 20 minutes. Going through intersections I, L and N, is 3 minutes. Total time is 23 minutes.

ETHICAL JUDGMENT

1. The Forgotten Evidence

    Correct Answer: C

    Difficulty: Hard

    Concept: Integrity / Court Procedure

This is the only option that maintains absolute integrity. Admitting a mistake damages credibility slightly, but lying or altering notes (fabricating evidence) destroys it permanently and is a criminal offense. The Crown must know the weaknesses of the case.

Why choice A is incorrect: Backdating notes is falsifying records. It is illegal and an immediate firing offense.
Why choice B is incorrect: Withholding relevant evidence (omission) is unethical and violates disclosure laws.
Why choice D is incorrect: Perjury. Lying under oath is a criminal offense.

2. The Sick Day

    Correct Answer: B

    Difficulty: Easy

    Concept: Accountability / Resource Management

Sick leave is an insurance benefit for illness, not extra vacation time. Abusing it reduces manpower and places a burden on partners who must cover the shift.

Why choice A is incorrect: This is a common misconception, but ethically and contractually, sick time is for incapacity to work.
Why choices C & D are incorrect: C involves deception. D implies calling in sick is a backup plan, which is premeditated misuse of leave.

3. The Excessive Force Witness

    Correct Answer: C

    Difficulty: Hard

    Concept: Duty to Intervene / Accountability

Police officers have a legal and ethical "Duty to Intervene" when they witness excessive force. Safety is the priority. Reporting it immediately is required by integrity standards.

Why choice A is incorrect: The "Blue Wall of Silence." Protecting a partner who commits assault makes you an accessory to the crime.
Why choice B is incorrect: Falsifying a report is a criminal offense (Obstruction of Justice).
Why choice D is incorrect: It shifts the burden to the victim and ignores your duty to report misconduct.

4. The Background Check

Correct Answer: B
Difficulty: Easy
Concept: Misuse of Information / CPIC Policy

Accessing police databases (like CPIC) for personal reasons is one of the most common reasons for officer dismissal and criminal charges. Strict refusal is the only option.

Why choice A is incorrect: This is a criminal offense (Breach of Trust).
Why choice C is incorrect: This involves a colleague in your misconduct, endangering their career as well.
Why choice D is incorrect: While PIs exist, you shouldn't facilitate the "investigation" of a private citizen based on gossip. However, B is the stronger ethical stance regarding your own duty.

5. The Impaired Colleague

Correct Answer: B
Difficulty: Hard
Concept: Public Safety / Duty to Act

Why choice B is correct: Immediate public safety overrides professional courtesy. You must try to stop the offense before it happens. If they refuse, they are a danger to the public, and 911 is the fastest resource.

Why choice A is incorrect: Calling a supervisor might take too long; the drunk driver will be on the road by the time a unit is dispatched.
Why choice C is incorrect: Reporting it "the next morning" allows a drunk driver to be on the road tonight, potentially killing someone.
Why choice D is incorrect: Officers have a sworn duty to preserve life, regardless of who the offender is.

6. The Inappropriate Joke

Correct Answer: D
Difficulty: Medium
Concept: Workplace Harassment / Leadership / Courage

This is the most professional approach. It does not validate the behavior (by laughing) but avoids a public shouting match which disrupts discipline. However, it addresses the issue directly and firmly. If it persists, reporting is necessary.

Why choice A is incorrect: Complicity. Laughing makes you part of the problem.
Why choice B is incorrect: Passive avoidance does not fix the toxic culture.
Why choice C is incorrect: While the sentiment is right, public confrontation can escalate effectively. A measured, private, or formal approach is usually preferred unless the behavior is dangerous.

7. The Domestic Call Bias

Correct Answer: A
Difficulty: Medium
Concept: Rule of Law / Impartiality

In Canada, police have very little discretion regarding Domestic Violence (DV). If grounds exist, an arrest must be made ("Mandatory Charge" policies). Political status is irrelevant.

Why choice B is incorrect:"Separating parties" when grounds for assault exist violates DV policy and leaves the victim at risk.
Why choice C is incorrect:You do not need the Chief's permission to enforce the law; asking suggests you think the politician is above the law.
Why choice D is incorrect:False arrest and corruption.

8. The Found Wallet

> Correct Answer: C
> Difficulty: Easy
> Concept: Integrity / Theft

All property found must be logged. It is the only legal way to handle it.

Why choice A is incorrect:Theft by finding. Being poor does not justify theft.
Why choice B is incorrect:Neglect of duty. An officer should secure property.
Why choice D is incorrect:It is not your money to donate.

9. The Mental Health Crisis

Correct Answer: C
Difficulty: Hard
Concept: Use of Force / De-escalation (Gavin De-escalation Model)

The subject is contained (distance), not immediately threatening anyone (non-aggressive posture), and clearly in crisis. The priority is preservation of life. Time is on your side. De-escalation and waiting for specialized resources (like a crisis team) is the standard best practice.

Why choice A is incorrect: Lethal force is only justified if there is an imminent threat of death or grievous bodily harm. He is 20 feet away and not advancing.
Why choice B is incorrect: Immediate Taser deployment without trying to talk first (when safe to do so) is excessive. It can also escalate the situation.
Why choice D is incorrect: Rushing a person with a knife is tactically reckless and endangers your life unnecessarily.

10. The Courtroom Error

Correct Answer: C
Difficulty: Medium
Concept: Integrity / Court Procedure

Human memory is fallible, but integrity must be absolute. Correcting the record immediately shows honesty. The court accepts that officers rely on notes. Hiding the mistake is worse than the mistake itself.

Why choice A is incorrect: Knowing your testimony is false and refusing to correct it constitutes perjury.
Why choice B is incorrect: You cannot speak to a Judge privately about a case; this is "ex parte communication" and violates legal procedure.
Why choice D is incorrect: Lying by saying "I don't recall" when you do recall is perjury.

11. The Supervisor's Request

Correct Answer: C
Difficulty: Easy
Concept: Integrity / Accountability

You cannot legally witness something you didn't see. Signing a legal document falsely is fraud. However, offering to help in other ways shows you are a team player and respectful, despite the refusal.
Why choice A is incorrect: Blind obedience to an unethical

request makes you liable for fraud.
Why choice B is incorrect: Reporting immediately without a conversation is "jumping the gun." A refusal usually solves the issue.
Why choice D is incorrect: Even with the note, your signature implies you are the witnessing officer. It creates a confusing legal document.

12. The Racial Profiling Suspicions

Correct Answer: B
Difficulty: Medium
Concept: Human Rights / Bias-Free Policing

"Driving while Black/Brown" is not a crime. Police need reasonable suspicion of an offense to detain someone. This is a clear human rights violation. You have a duty to prevent your partner from violating rights.

Why choice A is incorrect: "Intuition" based on race is bias. Following it makes you complicit in racial profiling.
Why choice C is incorrect: Politeness does not cure an unlawful detention.
Why choice D is incorrect: Silence is complicity.

13. The Spilled Evidence

Correct Answer: C
Difficulty: Medium
Concept: Evidence Handling / Integrity

Transparency is key. You must document exactly what happened so the court understands why the weight might be different or why the sample is dirty. This preserves the "Chain of Custody" and credibility.

Why choice A is incorrect: Contaminating evidence makes it inadmissible.
Why choice B is incorrect: You cannot destroy evidence, even if it is spilled.
Why choice D is incorrect: Fabricating evidence (adding baking soda) is a serious criminal offense (Obstruction of Justice).

14. The Counter-Protest

Correct Answer: B
Difficulty: Medium
Concept: Public Order / Charter Rights

Police must remain neutral. Your job is to facilitate peaceful protest for all sides while maintaining order. Separation is the standard tactic.

Why choice A is incorrect: Counter-protesters have the same right to free speech as the main group, provided they are peaceful.
Why choice C is incorrect: Mass arrest without specific criminal acts is unlawful.
Why choice D is incorrect: Reactive rather than proactive. Waiting for violence risks injury.

15. The Off-Duty Robbery

Correct Answer: C
Difficulty: Hard
Concept: Use of Force / Off-Duty Safety

"Be a good witness." Intervening with a firearm in a crowded store is extremely high risk (crossfire, mistaken identity by arriving police). Property (cash) is not worth a life. Intervention is reserved for immediate threats to life (e.g., stabbing starts).

Why choice A is incorrect: Escalation. Drawing a gun on a robber might cause a shoot-out, endangering your family and the clerk.
Why choice B is incorrect: Physically engaging an armed man while off-duty (no radio, no vest, no backup) is tactically unsound.
Why choice D is incorrect: Might startle the gunman into shooting.

PRACTICE TEST QUESTIONS 2

Ready to Test Your Skills? Below you will find a full-length practice test. Please note that these are not the exact questions from the official exam—those are kept secret and change every year. Instead, we have created questions that mirror the style and difficulty of the official test.

The Bottom Line: If you can answer these questions correctly, you have the knowledge needed to pass the real exam.
Instructions:

Get in the Zone: Set aside uninterrupted time in a quiet room.

Focus: Read the instructions and every question carefully. Answer to the best of your ability.

Simulate: Use the provided bubble answer sheets to mimic the real test experience.

Review: Once finished, check your work against the Answer Key and read the explanations for any questions you missed.

Pro Tip: Do not attempt more than one practice test in a single day. Rest is just as important as practice. Wait 48 to 72 hours between tests for maximum retention.

Spelling Answer Sheet

	A	B	C	D
1	○	○	○	○
2	○	○	○	○
3	○	○	○	○
4	○	○	○	○
5	○	○	○	○
6	○	○	○	○
7	○	○	○	○
8	○	○	○	○
9	○	○	○	○
10	○	○	○	○
11	○	○	○	○
12	○	○	○	○
13	○	○	○	○
14	○	○	○	○
15	○	○	○	○

Vocabulary Answer Sheet

       A   B   C   D
1.   ○   ○   ○   ○
2.   ○   ○   ○   ○
3.   ○   ○   ○   ○
4.   ○   ○   ○   ○
5.   ○   ○   ○   ○
6.   ○   ○   ○   ○
7.   ○   ○   ○   ○
8.   ○   ○   ○   ○
9.   ○   ○   ○   ○
10.   ○   ○   ○   ○
11.   ○   ○   ○   ○
12.   ○   ○   ○   ○
13.   ○   ○   ○   ○
14.   ○   ○   ○   ○
15.   ○   ○   ○   ○

Grammar & Punctuation Answer Sheet

	A	B	C	D
1	○	○	○	○
2	○	○	○	○
3	○	○	○	○
4	○	○	○	○
5	○	○	○	○
6	○	○	○	○
7	○	○	○	○
8	○	○	○	○
9	○	○	○	○
10	○	○	○	○
11	○	○	○	○
12	○	○	○	○
13	○	○	○	○
14	○	○	○	○
15	○	○	○	○

Rule Following Answer Sheet

	A	B	C	D
1	○	○	○	○
2	○	○	○	○
3	○	○	○	○
4	○	○	○	○
5	○	○	○	○
6	○	○	○	○
7	○	○	○	○
8	○	○	○	○
9	○	○	○	○
10	○	○	○	○
11	○	○	○	○
12	○	○	○	○
13	○	○	○	○
14	○	○	○	○
15	○	○	○	○

Mapping Answer Sheet

	A	B	C	D
1	○	○	○	○
2	○	○	○	○
3	○	○	○	○
4	○	○	○	○
5	○	○	○	○
6	○	○	○	○
7	○	○	○	○
8	○	○	○	○
9	○	○	○	○
10	○	○	○	○
11	○	○	○	○
12	○	○	○	○
13	○	○	○	○
14	○	○	○	○
15	○	○	○	○

Ethics Answer Sheet

	A	B	C	D
1	○	○	○	○
2	○	○	○	○
3	○	○	○	○
4	○	○	○	○
5	○	○	○	○
6	○	○	○	○
7	○	○	○	○
8	○	○	○	○
9	○	○	○	○
10	○	○	○	○
11	○	○	○	○
12	○	○	○	○
13	○	○	○	○
14	○	○	○	○
15	○	○	○	○

Section A Language

Spelling

1. A) Warrant B) Warrent C) Warant D) Warent

2. A) Manoeuvre B) Manuver C) Manouver D) Manuever

3. A) Offence B) Offense C) Ofence D) Offens

4. A) Recieve B) Receive C) Receve D) Recicve

5. A) Argument B) Arguement C) Argumint D) Argue-ment

6. A) Publically B) Publicly C) Publicaly D) Publicley

7. A) Consensis B) Consensus C) Concensus D) Consencus

8. A) Deductible B) Deductable C) Deducteble D) Diductible

9. A) Breathalyzer B) Breathalizer C) Brethelyzer D) Breathalyser

10. A) Marijuanna B) Marijuana C) Mariguana D) Marijauna

11. A) Misdemeanor B) Misdemenor C) Misdeameanor D) Misdemener

12. A) Perjury B) Perjurey C) Purgery D) Purjury

13. A) Trespass B) Trespas C) Tresspass D) Tresspas

14. A) Superintendent B) Superintendant C) Suprintendent D) Superentendent

15. A) Possession B) Posesion C) Posession D) Possesion

VOCABULARY

1. The suspect was carrying a **lethal** weapon.

   A) Hidden
   B) Deadly
   C) Stolen
   D) Fake

2. The witness received a **subpoena** to appear in court next Tuesday.

   A) Invitation
   B) Summons
   C) Fine
   D) Letter

3. You have the right to **waive** your right to legal counsel.

   A) Demand
   B) Use
   C) Forgo
   D) Understand

4. The chemicals found in the lab were deemed **hazardous** to the public.

   A) Expensive
   B) Dangerous
   C) Useful
   D) Accessible

5. He was charged with **obstruction** of justice for hiding the evidence.

    A) Hindrance
    B) Support
    C) Ignorance
    D) Knowledge

6. The coroner arrived to examine the **deceased**.

    A) Evidence
    B) Dead person
    C) Injured person
    D) Scene

7. Police responded to a verbal **altercation** at the local bar.

    A) Agreement
    B) Dispute
    C) Party
    D) Meeting

8. It is a crime to **brandish** a weapon in a public place.

    A) Carry
    B) Wave threateningly
    C) Buy
    D) Hide

9. The **fugitive** was finally caught after a three-day manhunt.

    A) Prisoner
    B) Runaway
    C) Thief
    D) Spy

10. The court provides legal aid for **indigent** defendants who cannot afford a lawyer.

    A) Guilty
    B) Angry
    C) Poor
    D) Young

11. The vandal was ordered to pay **restitution** for the broken windows.

    A) Taxes
    B) Compensation
    C) Attention
    D) Homage

12. The jury delivered a **verdict** of not guilty.

    A) Question
    B) Sentence
    C) Decision
    D) Speech

13. The goal of the defense is to **acquit** the accused of all charges.

    A) Clear
    B) Convict
    C) Punish
    D) Ignore

14. Programs are in place to reduce criminal **recidivism** among youth.

  A) Activity
  B) Reoffending
  C) Employment
  D) Education

15. His arguments were **specious**.

  A) Logical
  B) Illogical
  C) Emotional
  D) None of the above

Grammar and Punctuation

1. Identify the error in this sentence: "Each of the officers need to file a report."

  A) Punctuation error
  B) Subject-verb agreement error
  C) Spelling error
  D) No error

2. Which sentence uses parallel structure correctly?

  A) The duties include patrolling, reporting, and to interview witnesses.
  B) The duties include to patrol, reporting, and interviewing witnesses.
  C) The duties include patrolling, reporting, and interviewing witnesses.
  D) The duties include patrol, report, and interviewing witnesses.

3. Choose the correct sentence.

A) Neither the sergeant nor the constables was available.

B) Neither the sergeant nor the constables were available.

C) Neither the sergeant or the constables were available.

D) Neither the sergeant nor the constables is available.

4. Which sentence avoids a "dangling modifier"?

A) To get a better view, the binoculars were adjusteD)
B) Adjusted for a better view, the suspect was clearly visible.

C) To get a better view, the officer adjusted the binoculars.

D) Upon entering the room, the weapon was founD)

5. The criteria for the warrant _____ not met.

A) was
B) were
C) is
D) has been

6. We observed the suspect _____ the building.

A) entered
B) enter
C) enters
D) entering into

7. The logic of his argument is different _____ hers.

    A) than
    B) from
    C) to
    D) then

8. _____ did you speak to at the precinct?

    A) Who
    B) Whom
    C) Whose
    D) Which

5. The data _____ collected over six months.

    A) was
    B) were
    C) is
    D) has been

10. Which sentence correctly handles the list?

    A) We need to interview Mr. Smith, the neighbor; Ms. Jones, the landlord; and Dave, the superintendent.

    B) We need to interview Mr. Smith, the neighbor, Ms. Jones, the landlord, and Dave, the superintendent.

    C) We need to interview Mr. Smith; the neighbor, Ms. Jones; the landlord, and Dave; the superintendent.

    D) We need to interview Mr. Smith, the neighbor: Ms. Jones, the landlord: and Dave, the superintendent.

11. Identify the error:

A) Its' color was reD)

B) It's time to go.

C) Its color was reD)

D) They're waiting outside.

12. Which sentence uses quotation marks correctly?

A) The Sergeant said that "we should wait for the warrant." B) The Sergeant said, "We should wait for the warrant."

C) The Sergeant said "We should wait for the warrant".

D) The Sergeant said "we should wait for the warrant."

13. Choose the correctly punctuated address.

A) He lived at 123 Main St., Toronto, Ontario.

B) He lived at 123 Main St. Toronto Ontario.

C) He lived at 123, Main St., Toronto, Ontario.

D) He lived at 123 Main St.; Toronto, Ontario.

14. Elaine promised to bring the camera _____ at the mall yesterday.

A) by me
B) with me
C) at me
D) to me

15. Following the tornado, telephone poles _____ all over the street.

A) laid
B) lied
C) were lying
D) were laying

Section B: Police Problem Solving

Rule Application

Instructions: For each set of questions, read the provided "Rules and Definitions" carefully. Answer the questions based ONLY on the information provided in the rules. Do not use outside knowledge of actual laws.

Property Offenses Classifications
Definitions:

Theft: Occurs when a person fraudulently and without color of right takes, or fraudulently converts to his/her own use, anything with intent to deprive the owner of it.

Robbery: Occurs when a person steals, and for the purpose of extorting whatever is stolen or to prevent or overcome resistance to the stealing, uses violence or threats of violence to a person or property.

Break and Enter: Occurs when a person enters a place with intent to commit an indictable offense therein. "Place" includes a dwelling-house, building, or structure.

Mischief: Occurs when a person willfully destroys or damages property, renders property dangerous, useless, inoperative, or ineffective, or obstructs, interrupts, or interferes with the lawful use, enjoyment, or operation of property.

1. A suspect pushes a pedestrian to the ground and snatches her purse, then runs away. Based on the rules, this is:

   A) Theft
   B) Robbery
   C) Mischief
   D) Break and Enter

2. A suspect uses a specialized tool to jam a subway turnstile so it will not spin, preventing people from entering. He takes no money. Based on the rules, this is:

A) Mischief
B) Theft
C) Robbery
D) Break and Enter

3. A person sees a laptop sitting on a park bench. Thinking no one is looking, he takes it and brings it home. Based on the rules, this is:

A) Mischief
B) Robbery
C) Break and Enter
D) Theft

4. A suspect breaks a window of a jewelry store, reaches in, and grabs a watch. He does not fully enter the store. (Note: Refer strictly to the definitions provided). The most accurate classification among the choices is:

A) Mischief (due to the broken window)
B) Robbery (due to the force on the window)
C) Theft (due to taking the watch)
D) Break and Enter (due to breaking the barrier)

Rule Set 2: Traffic Enforcement & Towing Protocol Rules:

    1. Ticket (Offense Notice): Issued for minor moving violations (speeding less than 30 km/h over limit, failing to stop) or minor document errors (expired license less than 1 month).

    2. Summons: Issued for major violations (speeding 30 km/h or more over limit, No Insurance) or repeat offenders.

    3. Verbal Warning: Issued only for equipment violations (broken taillight) where the driver agrees to fix it within 24 hours.

    4. Vehicle Impoundment (Towing): Mandatory if the driver has a suspended license OR is speeding 50 km/h or more over the limit.

    5. License Seizure: Mandatory if the driver has a suspended license.

5. A driver is speeding 55 km/h over the limit. The officer issues a Summons. What else must happen?

    A) The license must be seized.

    B) The vehicle must be impounded.

    C) The driver must be given a verbal warning.

    D) Nothing else.

6. A driver has a broken headlight (equipment violation) but refuses to say they will fix it. Can the officer issue a Verbal Warning based on the rules?

    A) Yes, because it is an equipment violation.

    B) No, because the driver did not agree to fix it.

    C) Yes, if the driver has a valid license.

    D) No, unless they are also speeding.

7. A driver is stopped for speeding 35 km/h over the limit. The driver asks for a ticket instead of a summons. Can the officer grant this request based on the rules?

A) Yes, speeding is a moving violation.

B) No, speeding 30 km/h or more requires a Summons.

C) Yes, if the driver has insurance.

D) No, the vehicle must be impounded.

Rule Set 3: Use of Force Continuum

Rules:

Level 1 (Officer Presence): Use when subject is cooperative.

Level 2 (Verbal Communication): Use when subject is passively resistant (refusing to move, ignoring commands) but not physical.

Level 3 (Soft Physical Control): (Holds, joint locks) Use when subject is actively resistant (pulling away, running away) but not attacking.

Level 4 (Hard Physical Control): (Strikes, baton) Use when subject is assaultive (kicking, punching, biting) causing risk of bodily harm.

Level 5 (Lethal Force): Use when subject poses a threat of death or grievous bodily harm to officer or public.

8. An officer tells a crowd to disperse. One person shouts "No!" but stays standing still. What level is this behavior classified as?

A) Cooperative

B) Passively Resistant

C) Actively Resistant

D) Assaultive

9. Using a baton to strike a suspect is considered which level of control?

   A) Verbal Communication

   B) Soft Physical Control

   C) Hard Physical Control

   D) Lethal Force

10. A suspect pushes an officer and raises a fist to strike again. The officer uses a joint lock (Soft Physical). Is this within the rules?

   A) No, the officer used too much force.

   B) Yes, the officer can always use a lower level than authorized.

   C) No, the officer must use Lethal Force.

   D) Yes, but only if the suspect has a weapon.

11. Active resistance is best described in the rules as:

   A) Ignoring commands.

   B) Pulling away or running.

   C) Attacking the officer.

   D) Following instructions.

12. A suspect is holding a baseball bat and threatening to break a car window (property), but is not threatening any person. Is Level 5 authorized?

   A) Yes, because he has a weapon.

   B) No, because there is no threat of death or grievous bodily harm to a person.

   C) Yes, to protect the property.

   D) No, only Level 2 is authorized

Rule Set 4: Public Park Bylaws

Rules:

Zone A (Playground): Open 9:00 AM to Sundown. No dogs allowed. No alcohol.

Zone B (Picnic Area): Open 8:00 AM to 11:00 PM. Dogs allowed on leash. Alcohol allowed with permit.

Zone C (Trails): Open Sunrise to Sunset. Dogs allowed off-leash. No alcohol. No bicycles.

Enforcement:

Violation of Hours: $100 Fine.

Violation of Alcohol Policy: $200 Fine.

Violation of Dog Policy: $50 Fine.

13. A person is drinking wine in Zone C at 4:00 PM. They have a permit. Is this allowed?

A) Yes, because they have a permit.

B) No, alcohol is never allowed in Zone C.

C) Yes, because it is before Sunset.

D) No, unless they also have a dog.

14. It is 7:00 AM. A person is sitting in Zone B. What is the fine?

A) $50

B) $100

C) $200

D) No violation

15. Which Zone allows dogs to run free (off-leash)?

   A) Zone A
   B) Zone B
   C) Zone C
   D) All Zones

Mapping

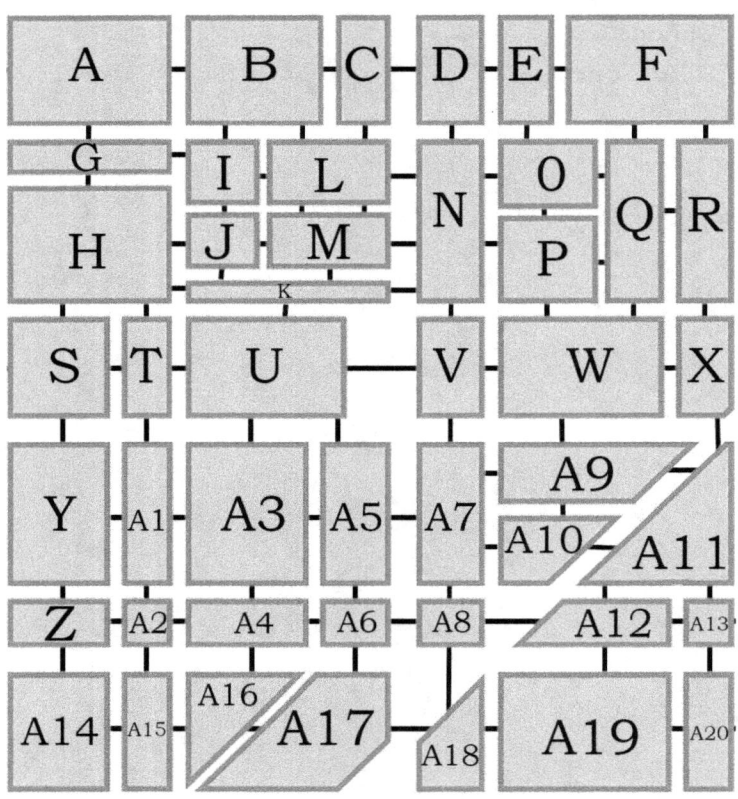

Map Key

Each Square labeled A to Z and A1 to A20 represent the corner of an intersection. The lines between the squares represent a city block. The intersections and city blocks fall into 3 categories.

Large blocks: A, B,F, H, N, Q, R, U, W, Y, A3, A5, A7, A9, A11, A14, A17, A19

Small blocks: C, D, E, I. J, L,M, O, P, S, T, V, X, A, A1, A4, A10, Z, A12, A15, A16, A18, A20
Mini blocks: G, K, A2, A6, A8, A13
The time it takes to travel from one city block to another is:

Large blocks

In a car: 4 minutes
On a bike: 6 minutes
On foot: 10 minutes

Small Blocks

In a car: 3 minutes
On a bike: 5 minutes
On foot: 8 minutes

Mini Blocks

In a car: 2 minutes
On a bike: 4 minutes
On foot: 6 minutes

1. A girl rides a bike from A12 to A5 and returns to A12 by a different route. How long would it take?

    A) 35 minutes

    B) 37 minutes

    C) 39 minutes

    D) 28 minutes

2. There is a parade and block O is closed to vehicles. A driver starts at block N and drives to R. Then he has to return to N by a different route. How fast could he accomplish this?

   A) 20 minutes
   B) 11 minutes
   C) 27 minutes
   D) 25 minutes

3. A man rides a bike from A18 to block N and then returns via the same route. How long would it take him if he used the fastest route?

   A) 41 minutes
   B) 38 minutes
   C) 44 minutes
   D) 29 minutes

4. A police patrol team drove from A3 to A10, with a 30 seconds stop at each intersection in between. From A10 it then drove to block W without spending any extra time at the intersections. How long would the trip take using the fastest route?

   A) 19 minutes, 30 seconds
   B) 18 minutes
   C) 20 minutes
   D) 21 minutes, 45 seconds

5. A delivery van goes from block U to A4. How fast would it take, it if it had to go through block V and spend an extra 15 seconds each time it has to make a turn at an intersection?

   A) 15 minutes, 30 seconds
   B) 15 minutes, 15 seconds
   C) 17 minutes, 30 seconds
   D) 16 minutes, 30 seconds

6. A group of 4 students move from block F to block A) How fast can they go if they drive a car the first 2 blocks, ride their bikes the next 2 blocks and walk the rest of the way?

   A) 25 minutes
   B) 27 minutes
   C) 30 minutes
   D) 29 minutes

7. A car drives from block R to A10. Using the fastest route, how long would it take if it spends 30 seconds each time it has to turn at an intersection?

   A) 6 minutes
   B) 7 minutes
   C) 10 minutes, 30 seconds
   D) 7 minutes, 30 seconds

8. Using the fastest route, a bike ride from V to A18 and then a car ride to A4 through A16 would take how long?

   A) 25 minutes
   B) 22 minutes
   C) 28 minutes
   D) 24 minutes

9. A boy rides his bike from S to K but gets lost along the way. What is the shortest time it would have taken him if his trip took him through blocks J and L?

   A) 20 minutes
   B) 22 minutes
   C) 23 minutes
   D) 25 minutes

10. Which of the following would be the shortest trip?

    A) Bike ride from D to V

    B) Walking from O to W

    C) Driving a car from B to A3

    D) They all take the same time

11. A bike race starts from block U and finishes at block A18. If the race has to pass through blocks V and A6, what is the shortest possible time to complete the race?

    A) 29 minutes

    B) 34 minutes

    C) 30 minutes

    D) 31 minutes

12. There is traffic congestion around blocks N, V, A7 and A8. Cars can't get through, and drivers need to park and walk. A car driver heads for block A12 from U. How quickly can they get there?

    A) 19 minutes

    B) 17 minutes

    C) 21 minutes

    D) 18 minutes

13. How long will it take to walk from block T to block A15 if you must walk through A16?

    A) 38 minutes

    B) 41 minutes

    C) 42 minutes

    D) 37 minutes

14. How long will it take to drive a car from S to W?

   A) 6 minutes
   B) 12 minutes
   C) 18 minutes
   D) 13 minutes

15. How long to ride a bike from block G to block O?

   A) 24 minutes
   B) 19 minutes
   C) 20 minutes
   D) 1 minutes

ETHICAL JUDGMENT

1. The Homeless Trespasser A shop owner calls the police to remove a homeless individual sleeping in their doorway. It is a bitterly cold night, and the shelters are full. The individual is cooperative but has nowhere to go. The shop owner insists on pressing trespassing charges.
What is the best course of action?

   A) Arrest the individual for trespassing as the shop owner requests; the law is the law.

   B) Drive the individual to a neighboring jurisdiction and drop them off near a 24-hour coffee shop.

   C) Attempt to mediate with the shop owner to allow the person to stay until morning, or help the individual find a safe alternative location/transport to a warming center before considering charges.

   D) Tell the shop owner you cannot arrest someone for being homeless and leave the scene.

2. The Old Friend You are investigating a series of break-and-enters. You find security footage that clearly shows the perpetrator is a close childhood friend you haven't seen in years. What is the best course of action?

A) Continue the investigation yourself to be sure, then arrest them quietly to minimize their embarrassment.

B) Immediately recuse yourself from the case, report the conflict of interest to your supervisor, and hand over the evidence.

C) Call your friend to encourage them to turn themselves in before you file the report.

D) Ignore the footage if the image is blurry enough to be argued in court.

3. The Informant's Gift A confidential informant who has provided information leading to major arrests offers you a generic gift card worth $50 as a "Christmas present." They say no one has ever treated them with as much respect as you have. What is the best response?

A) Accept the gift to maintain the rapport, as rejecting it might damage the relationship.

B) Accept the gift but donate it to a police charity.

C) Politely decline the gift, explaining that professional standards prevent you from accepting it, but acknowledge their sentiment.

D) Accept the gift but report it to your supervisor immediately.

PRACTICE TEST QUESTIONS 2   145

4. The Bylaw Dispute (Level 2 - Medium Difficulty)
You are dispatched to a noise complaint. It is your neighbor's house. The neighbor is having a party that is slightly over the noise limit, but it is their 50th birthday. What is the best course of action?

> A) Advise dispatch of the conflict of interest and request another unit to attend.
>
> B) Go to the house, tell them to keep it down, and mark the call as resolved without logging their details.
>
> C) Ignore the call; they are your neighbors and you have to live next to them.
>
> D) Attend the house and issue a ticket immediately to prove you are unbiased.

5. The Prisoner's Medication (Level 2 - Medium) You are processing a prisoner who is being verbally abusive and spitting at the glass of the holding cell. The prisoner claims they need their heart medication, which is in their personal property bag. You suspect they just want attention, but you are not a doctor. What is the best course of action?

> A) Ignore the request until they calm down and stop being abusive; rewarding bad behavior sets a bad precedent.
>
> B) Give them the medication immediately to make them be quiet.
>
> C) Consult the Officer in Charge (Staff Sergeant) or call for paramedics to assess the medical need, regardless of the prisoner's behavior.
>
> D) Tell the prisoner they forfeited their right to medication when they started spitting.

6. The Social Media Evidence You are investigating a gang assault. You find a public Facebook photo of the suspect holding a weapon similar to the one used in the crime. You want to save this evidence before the suspect deletes it. What is the best course of action?

A) Use your personal phone to screenshot the image and email it to your work account.

B) Create a fake profile to send a friend request to the suspect to see more private photos.

C) Follow your Service's procedure for capturing open-source intelligence (OSINT) to ensure the evidence is admissible and the chain of custody is preserved.

D) Print the photo and put it in the file, but don't mention where it came from in your report.

7. The Free Meal Policy (Level 2 - Medium) Your police service has a strict policy against accepting free food (gratuities). You are in line at a fast-food place, and the cashier hands you your meal, saying, "Manager says no charge." There is a long line behind you, and arguing might cause a delay. What is the best course of action?

A) Take the food and put the cash equivalent in the charity box on the counter.

B) Politely but firmly insist on paying, explaining that policy prevents you from accepting.

C) Accept the food this one time to keep the line moving, but don't come back.

D) Accept the food and tell your supervisor later that you "saved the department money" on a meal break.

8. The Rookie's Mistake You are a training officer. Your rookie partner makes a mistake during a traffic stop that violates a minor procedure but does not violate the law or rights of the driver. The driver does not notice. What is the best course of action?

    A) Embarrass the rookie in front of the driver to ensure they never do it again.

    B) Say nothing; it's a minor issue and they will learn eventually.

    C) Debrief the rookie privately after the stop is concluded to correct the behavior and ensure they understand the proper procedure.

    D) Write the rookie up formally for incompetence.

9. The Victim's Date You helped a victim of a break-in feel safe and secure while processing the scene. A week later, the victim contacts you on your work email thanking you and asking if you would like to go out for dinner as a date. What is the best response?

    A) Accept the date; the case is closed and you are two consenting adults.

    B) Decline politely, explaining that professional ethics prevent officers from dating victims or witnesses involved in their cases.

    C) Ignore the email and block the address.

    D) Report the victim for harassment.

10. The "Blue Wall" Pressure (Level 3 - High Difficulty)
You are interviewed by Internal Affairs regarding a complaint of theft against your best friend on the force. You know your friend took money from a crime scene because he confessed it to you in confidence. He begs you not to ruin his life over "one mistake." What is the best course of action?

> A) Tell Internal Affairs you know nothing; loyalty to your partner is the most important thing in policing.
>
> B) Tell your friend to resign immediately so you don't have to testify.
>
> C) Refuse to answer questions claiming "protection of a private conversation."
>
> D) Truthfully disclose what you know to Internal Affairs; your duty to the public and the law supersedes personal loyalty.

11. The Media Leak You are guarding a perimeter at a high-profile murder scene. A reporter you know approaches you and asks for "off the record" details about the victim's identity, promising it will help solve the case by getting the word out. The victim's family has not been notified yet. What is the best response?

> A) Give the reporter the name strictly "off the record" to help the investigation.
>
> B) Politely decline to comment and direct them to the designated Media Relations Officer.
>
> C) Give them a fake name to throw them off the trail and protect the family.
>
> D) Threaten to arrest the reporter for obstruction of justice if they don't leave.

12. The Overtime Padding You and your partner finish a call at 3:45 PM. Your shift ends at 4:00 PM. Your partner says, "If we stay here and write the notes until 4:15 PM, we get paid for a minimum 3 hours of overtime per union rules. Let's hang tight." What is the best course of action?

A) Agree; you are underpaid anyway and the contract allows it.

B) Return to the station and clock out at 4:00 PM; deliberately delaying work to claim unearned overtime is theft of time.

C) Sit in the car but tell your partner you won't claim the overtime personally.

D) Drive back slowly so you naturally arrive at 4:05 PM.

13. The Road Rage (Off-Duty) You are off-duty driving your personal vehicle. Another driver cuts you off and gives you the finger. You are angry. What is the best course of action?

A) Follow the vehicle to get the license plate, then look it up on the police database later to see who it is.

B) Flash your badge out the window to scare them into slowing down.

C) Ignore the insult, maintain safe driving distance, and continue to your destination; de-escalating applies off-duty as well.

D) Honk your horn and pull up beside them to verbally reprimand them for dangerous driving.

14. The Unlawful Order (Level 2 - Medium) During a protest, your Incident Commander orders the unit to "Kettle" (box in) a group of peaceful protesters and arrest them all for breach of peace, even though they are obeying directions and staying on the sidewalk. You believe this order violates their Charter rights. What is the best course of action?

A) Follow the order blindly; soldiers and police must obey the chain of command above all else.

B) Respectfully state your concern to the Commander that the grounds for arrest do not exist; if the order stands, you may have to refuse to participate in an unlawful arrest.

C) Perform the arrests but apologize to the protesters while doing it.

D) Feign an injury to leave the line and avoid the situation.

15. The Chief's Daughter (The "Final Boss" Scenario)
You stop a vehicle for weaving across lanes at 2:00 AM. The driver is obviously intoxicated. When you ask for ID, you realize it is the daughter of your Police Chief. She says, "My dad is going to be so mad, please just let me call him to pick me up." What is the best course of action?

A) Call the Chief personally and ask what he wants you to do; it's his daughter.

B) Conduct the standard impaired driving investigation (breathalyzer, arrest if faileD) exactly as you would for any other citizen, and notify your supervisor of the sensitive identity only after the process is secure.

C) Drive her home and park her car; arresting the Chief's daughter is "career suicide."

D) Issue a 24-hour suspension instead of a criminal charge to balance safety with professional self-preservation.

Answer Key and Explanations

Section A - Language

Spelling

1. A) Warrant

Tip: War - rant. The suffix is -ant.

2. A) Manoeuvre

Tip: This is the Canadian/British spelling (OACP standard). The American "Maneuver" is technically accepted in some places, but stick to the 're' ending for Canadian exams.

3. A) Offence

Tip: Canadian Spelling Rule: Nouns end in -ce (Offence, Defence), Verbs end in -se (Offense). Since the test usually asks for the noun (the crime), choose 'c'.

4. B) Receive

Tip: "I before E, except after C."

5. A) Argument

Tip: You drop the 'e' from "Argue" when adding "-ment". (Unlike "Judgment" where rules vary, Argument never has an 'e').

6. B) Publicly

Tip: One of the few words ending in -ic that adds -ly without adding 'al'. It is NOT Publically.

7. B) Consensus

Tip: It has to do with Sense, not Census. It means a "coming together of senses/minds".

8. A) Deductible

Tip: If you can take it away (deduct), it is deduct-ible.

9. A) Breathalyzer

Tip: Derived from "Analyze". Use 'y' and 'z'.

10. B) Marijuana

Tip: The 'j' makes an 'h' sound (Spanish origin), and it ends in -ana. Note: In official reports, "Cannabis" is often preferred now, but "Marijuana" still appears on spelling tests.

11. A) Misdemeanor

Tip: Mis - demeanor. "Mean" is inside the word.

12. A) Perjury

Tip: Lying under oath. Per - jury.

13. A) Trespass

Tip: One S at the start, Double S at the end.

14. A) Superintendent

Tip: Super - in - ten - dent. Just like Lieutenant, it ends in -dent.

15. A) Possession

Tip: It possesses a lot of S's. Double S twice (ss...ss).

Vocabulary

1. B) Deadly.
Lethal means sufficient to cause death.

2. B Summons.
A subpoena is a writ ordering a person to attend a court.

3. C Forgo.
Waive means to refrain from insisting on or using (a right or claim.

4. B Dangerous.
Hazardous means risky or dangerous.

5. A Hindrance.
Obstruction means the action of obstructing or the state of being obstructed.

6. B Dead person.
Deceased refers to a person who has recently died.

7. B Dispute.
An altercation is a noisy argument or disagreement, especially in public.

8. B Wave threateningly.
Brandish means to wave or flourish (something, especially a weapon as a threat.

9. B Runaway.
A fugitive is a person who has escaped from a place or is in hiding, especially to avoid arrest.

10. C Poor.
Indigent means poor or needy (often used in "indigent counsel" context.

11. B Compensation.
Restitution is the restoration of something lost or stolen to its proper owner, or recompense for injury or loss.

12. C Decision.
A verdict is a decision on a disputed issue in a civil or criminal case or an inquest.

13. A Clear.
Acquit means to free (someone from a criminal charge by a verdict of not guilty.

14. B Re-offending.
Recidivism is the tendency of a convicted criminal to reoffend.

15. B Specious
Seemingly well-reasoned or factual, but actually fallacious or insincere; strongly held but false.

GRAMMAR AND PUNCTUATION

1. B
Explanation: "Each" is a singular subject. Therefore, the verb must be singular ("needs," not "need").

2. C
Explanation: Parallel structure requires items in a list to share the same grammatical form. "Patrolling, reporting, and interviewing" are all gerunds (-ing form).

3. B
Explanation: With "Neither/nor," the verb agrees with the subject closest to it. "Constables" is plural, so the verb must be plural ("were").

4. C
Explanation: In A and B, the introductory phrases dangle because the subject (binoculars/suspect) is not the one doing the looking or adjusting. In C, the officer is the one getting the view.

5. B
Explanation: "Criteria" is the plural form of "criterion." Therefore, it takes the plural verb "were."

6. B
Explanation: With verbs of perception (observe, see, hear), we use the base form of the verb (enter) or the -ing form (entering). "Enter" fits best here as a completed action.

7. B
Explanation: The correct idiom is "different from," not "different than" or "different to."

8. B
Explanation: "Whom" is the object of the preposition "to." (To whom did you speak?) A trick: if you can answer with "him," use "Whom."

9. B
Explanation: In strict academic/formal testing, "data" is the plural of "datum." Therefore, "were" is correct.

10. A
Explanation: When items in a list contain commas themselves (e.g., "Mr. Smith, the neighbor"), you must use semicolons to separate the major items to avoid confusion.

11. A
Explanation: "Its'" is never a word. "It's" = it is. "Its" = possessive.

12. B
Explanation: A comma introduces the quote. Capitalize the first letter of a complete sentence within quotes. Punctuation goes inside the quotation marks.

13. A
Explanation: Commas separate the street from the city, and the city from the province.

14. D
The preposition 'to' in this sentence means give.

15. C
"Lie" means to recline, and does not take an object. 'Lay' means to place and does take an object. Peter lay the books on the table, or the telephone poles were lying on the road.

Section B: Police Problem Solving

Rule Application

1. B (Robbery)
The suspect used violence (pushing to the ground) to overcome resistance to the stealing.

Choice A, Theft, is incorrect. The use of force elevates theft to robbery.

2. A (Mischief)
He rendered property (turnstile) inoperative/ineffective and interfered with lawful operation.
Choice B, Theft, is incorrect. Nothing was taken.

3. D (Theft)
He took property fraudulently to convert to his own use.

Choice A, Mischief, is incorrect. Property was not damaged.
Choice B, Robbery, is incorrect. There was no violence or threat.

4. D (Break and Enter)
Legal definition of B&E usually includes "entering" as any part of the body breaking the plane (reaching in). He broke the barrier and entered (hand) with intent to steal.

Choice A, Mischief, is incorrect. While mischief occurred, B&E is the more serious substantive offense regarding the building.
Choice C, Theft, is incorrect. He did take the watch, but the context of breaking the window to get it classifies the event as a Break and Enter.

Study Tip: In "logic" sections, if an action fits multiple definitions, look for the most specific or serious one involving the structure of the scenario. B&E focuses on the entry and intent.

5. B (The vehicle must be impounded)
55 km/h over triggers Rule 4 (Impoundment for speeding 50+).

Choice A is incorrect. License seizure is for suspended drivers, not speeding (unless specified).

6. B (No, because the driver did not agree to fix it)
Rule 3 states Verbal Warning is issued only where the driver agrees to fix it.
Choice A is incorrect. The nature of the violation isn't enough; the agreement is the condition.

7. B (No, speeding 30 km/h or more requires a Summons)
The rules are rigid. Rule 2 states Summons is issued for 30+ km/h. There is no discretion listed in the rules.

Study Tip: Deductive logic tests require you to follow the "IF > THEN" strictures. Even if a cop could give a break in real life, if the rule says "Issued for X," you must select that option.

8. B (Passively Resistant)
The rule defines passive resistance as "refusing to move" or "ignoring commands" without physical action.

9. C (Hard Physical Control)
The rule lists "baton" under Level 4 definitions.

10. B (Yes, the officer can always use a lower level than authorized)
The Use of Force model sets a maximum appropriate force. If a suspect is assaultive (Level 4 allowed), the officer can choose to use a lower level (Level 3 joint lock) if they feel it will work. Logic dictates you cannot exceed the limit, but you can use less.

Choice A is incorrect. The officer did not use too much force; they used less than allowed.

11. B (Pulling away or running)
Explicitly defined in the Rule for Level 3.

12. B (No, because there is no threat of death or grievous bodily harm to a person)
Level 5 is strictly for threats to "officer or public" (people). Property damage (car window) does not authorize lethal force.

Choice A is incorrect. Possession of a weapon alone doesn't trigger Level 5 unless the threat is against a person.

Study Tip: Pay close attention to the difference between "Passive" (dead weight) and "Active" (pulling away) resistance. This is a common trap in police testing.

13. B (No, alcohol is never allowed in Zone C)
Zone C rule says "No alcohol." It does not say "No alcohol without permit." It is a blanket prohibition.

Choice A is incorrect. Permits are only mentioned for Zone B.

14. B ($100)
Zone B opens at 8:00 AM. Being there at 7:00 AM is a Violation of Hours ($100).

15. C (Zone C)
Zone C rule: "Dogs allowed off-leash."

Mapping

1. B
The fastest route is A12 – A8 – A6 – A5 which takes 14 minutes. To return, A5 – A7 – A10 – A11 – A12 takes 23 minutes. Total time is 37 minutes.

2. D
The route to R is, N – P – Q – R which takes 11 minutes. The route back, avoiding O, is R – X – W – V which takes 14 minutes. Total time is 25 minutes.

3. A
The fastest route is A18 – A8 – A7 – V – N – V – A7 – A8 – A18. Total time is 41 minutes.

4. C
The fastest route is A3 – A5 – A7 – A10, which takes 12 minutes. 30 seconds stop at A5 and A7 is one minute. From A10 - A9 – W takes 7 minutes. Total time is 20 minutes.

5. A
The fastest route from U to A4 through V, is U – V – A7 – A8 – A6 – A4 and it takes 15 minutes. The car makes a turn at V and A8, that is 30 seconds. Total is 15 minutes, 30 seconds.

6. B
The fastest route is F – E – D – C – B – A. The first 2 blocks by car will take 7 minutes. The next 2 blocks by bike will take 10 minutes, the last block on foot would take 10 minutes. Total time 27 minutes.

7. D
The fastest route is R – X – A11 – A10 and it takes 7 minutes by car. He makes a turn at A11 for 30 seconds. Total time is 7 minutes, 30 seconds.

8. A
The fastest route is V – A7 – A8 – A18. By bike would take 15 minutes. From A18 through A16 to A14 by car would go through A18 – A17 – A16 – A4. By car would take 10 minutes. Total time is 25 minutes.

9. C
The shortest route is S – H – J – I – L – M – K. By bike it would take 23 minutes.

10. D
From D to V by bike would take 16 minutes. Walking from O to W would take 16 minutes. From B to A3 by car would take 16 minutes. So all three routes would take same time.

11. D
The fastest route that goes through V and A6 is U – V – A7 – A8 – A6 – A17 – A18. By bike would take 31 minutes.
12. B
The fastest route is U – A5 – A6 – A8. By car it would take 11 minutes. Then on foot to A12 would take 6 minutes. Total time is 17 minutes.

13. A
Fastest route is T – A1 – A2 – A4 – A16 – A15. Time on foot is 38 minutes.

14. D
Best route is S – T – U – V – W in 13 minutes.

15. C
The fastest route is G – I – L – N – O, which would take 20 minutes by bike.

Ethical Judgment

1. The Homeless Trespasser
Correct Answer: C
Difficulty: Medium
Concept: Problem Solving / Community Safety / Discretion

This utilizes "Problem-Oriented Policing." It balances the shop owner's rights with the vulnerable person's safety. It seeks a long-term solution rather than a quick enforcement action.

Why A is incorrect: While legally permissible, it is "lawful but awful." It clogs the court system and doesn't solve the root issue.
Why B is incorrect: "Starlight tours" (dumping people elsewhere) is highly unethical and dangerous to the individual.
Why D is incorrect: The shop owner has a right to request removal of trespassers; refusing to act fails in your duty to the business owner.

2. The Old Friend
Correct Answer: B
Difficulty: Easy
Concept: Conflict of Interest

You cannot investigate someone you have a personal relationship with. Recusal is the standard procedure to ensure the investigation is unbiased and stands up in court.
Why A is incorrect: Your relationship compromises the chain of evidence and the interrogation.
Why C is incorrect: "Tipping off" a suspect, even a friend, is Obstruction of Justice.
Why D is incorrect: Destruction or ignoring of evidence is criminal misconduct.

3. The Informant's Gift
Correct Answer: C
Difficulty: Medium
Concept: Boundaries / Integrity

It maintains professional boundaries while preserving the rapport. Accepting gifts from informants blurs the line between professional duty and personal friendship/payment.
Why A is incorrect: Violates policy on gratuities and compromises the handler/informant relationship.
Why B is incorrect: You still accepted the gift. The destination of the gift doesn't cure the initial breach of policy.
Why D is incorrect: Accepting it first creates the problem. Reporting it is good, but declining it initially is better.

4. The Bylaw Dispute
Correct Answer: A
Difficulty: Medium
Concept: Conflict of Interest

You cannot be neutral with a neighbor. If you are lenient, the complainant is angry; if you are strict, your neighbor relationship is ruined. Another unit ensures impartiality.
Why B is incorrect: This is preferential treatment (corruption).
Why C is incorrect: Neglect of duty. You cannot ignore a dispatch call.
Why D is incorrect: Over-enforcement to prove a point is unjust to the citizen.

5. The Prisoner's Medication

Correct Answer: C
Difficulty: Medium
Concept: Duty of Care / Prisoner Safety

Officers have a "Duty of Care" for anyone in custody. You are not qualified to decide if they need the meds. Medical professionals or the Officer in Charge must make that call. Behavior does not negate the right to life/health.

Why choice A is incorrect: Withholding medication as punishment is a human rights violation and could lead to in-custody death.

Why choice B is incorrect: You should not dispense meds without verifying what they are and if they are safe/required at that moment.
Why choice D is incorrect:Incorrect. You cannot forfeit the right to medical attention.

6. The Social Media Evidence

Correct Answer: C
Difficulty: Hard
Concept: Procedural Law / Admissibility

Evidence collected improperly may be thrown out in court. Using verified OSINT tools/procedures ensures the time-stamp and authenticity are recorded legally.

Why choice A is incorrect:Sending evidence to personal accounts breaks the chain of custody and opens your personal device to subpoena.
Why choice B is incorrect:Creating fake profiles to interact with suspects ("Catfishing") is an undercover operation requiring judicial authorization or specific oversight.
Why choice D is incorrect:Failing to disclose the source is a disclosure violation (hiding evidence origins).

7. The Free Meal Policy

Correct Answer: B
Difficulty: Medium
Concept: Conflict of Interest / Public Perception

Adhering to policy is the priority. Public perception matters; people in line see a cop getting free stuff and assume corruption or favoritism.

Why choice A is incorrect:While well-intentioned, it still violates the "No Gratuity" policy.
Why choice C is incorrect:"Just this once" is the start of the slippery slope.
Why choice D is incorrect:Rationalizing rule-breaking.

8. The Rookie's Mistake

Correct Answer: C
Difficulty: Easy
Concept: Teamwork / Mentorship / Leadership

"Praise in public, correct in private." This builds the rookie's confidence while ensuring the mistake is fixed.

Why choice A is incorrect: Belittling colleagues destroys morale and team cohesion.
Why choice B is incorrect: Failing to correct mistakes leads to bad habits and potential liability later.
Why choice D is incorrect: Too harsh for a minor, first-time error.

9. The Victim's Date

Correct Answer: B
Difficulty: Medium
Concept: Power Dynamics / Professional Boundaries

There is an inherent power imbalance between police and victims. Dating a victim from a case can be seen as exploitation or a conflict of interest, even if the case is "closed."

Why choice A is incorrect: Violates ethical codes regarding exploiting professional contacts for personal gain/relationships.
Why choice C is incorrect: Rude and unnecessary. A professional explanation is required.
Why choice D is incorrect: Asking for a date is not necessarily harassment; reporting it is an overreaction unless they persist after being told no.

10. The "Blue Wall" Pressure

Correct Answer: D
Difficulty: Hard
Concept: Integrity / Conflict of Interest

A police officer's ultimate loyalty is to the public and the Code of Conduct, not to peers. Theft is a criminal offense. Failing to report it makes you an accessory.

Why choice A is incorrect: Lying to investigators is obstruction. It will result in you being fired and charged along with your friend.
Why choice B is incorrect: Resignation doesn't solve the crime that occurred.
Why choice C is incorrect: There is no "privilege" (like Attorney-Client privilege) between police officers regarding crimes.

11. The Media Leak

Correct Answer: B
Difficulty: Easy
Concept: Confidentiality / Media Relations

Next of Kin (NOK) notification is the priority. Releasing a name before the family knows is cruel and violates policy. Media inquiries should always go to the PIO (Public Information Officer).

Why choice A is incorrect: Leaks jeopardize the investigation and the family's welfare.
Why choice C is incorrect: Lying to the press destroys the Service's credibility.
Why choice D is incorrect: The reporter is doing their job; they are not obstructing justice simply by asking.

12. The Overtime Padding

Correct Answer: B
Difficulty: Medium
Concept: Integrity / Stewardship of Resources

This is theft of public funds. If the work is done, the shift is done.

Why choice A is incorrect: This is fraud.
Why choice C is incorrect: Allowing your partner to commit fraud while you watch makes you complicit.
Why choice D is incorrect: Deliberately slowing down is also a form of time theft/inefficiency.

13. The Road Rage (Off-Duty)

Correct Answer: C
Difficulty: Easy
Concept: Off-Duty Conduct / Emotional Intelligence

Officers are held to a higher standard. Engaging in road rage brings disrepute to the uniform. Ignoring it is the safest and most professional choice.

Why choice A is incorrect: Using police databases (CPIC) for personal disputes is a criminal offense.
Why choice B is incorrect: "Flashing the badge" for personal gain or intimidation is an abuse of authority.
Why choice D is incorrect: Escalating the conflict is dangerous and unprofessional.

14. The Unlawful Order

Correct Answer: B
Difficulty: Hard
Concept: Obedience to Orders / Legal Authority

Officers are required to obey lawful orders. If an order is manifestly unlawful (violating Charter rights without cause), the officer has a duty to question it. If they proceed, they can be held personally liable for the civil rights violation.

Why choice A is incorrect: The "Nuremberg Defense" (I was just following orders) does not apply to police if the order is clearly illegal.
Why choice C is incorrect: Being polite while violating rights does not validate the arrest.
Why choice D is incorrect: This is cowardice and avoidance, not ethical decision making.

15. The Chief's Daughter

Correct Answer: B
Difficulty: Hard
Concept: Integrity / Impartiality

This is the ultimate test of integrity. The law applies to everyone equally. Special treatment for the "boss's daughter" is corruption. However, notifying a supervisor is prudent purely for internal communication (no surprises), but not for permission.

Why A is wrong: Seeking permission implies you would let her go if he said so. It puts the Chief in a compromised position.
Why C is wrong: Criminal Corruption/Obstruction of Justice.
Why D is wrong: "sweeping it under the rug" is a fireable offense.

PART 2: OACP CERTIFICATE SPECIFICS

PERSONALITY ASSESSMENT ESQ2 / SIGMA

What is the ESQ2?
The OACP Certificate process utilizes the Employment Screening Questionnaire 2 (ESQ2), often referred to as the Sigma Survey. Unlike the cognitive tests (like the SSIG) which measure ability (can you solve this problem?), the ESQ2 measures propensity (how are you likely to behave?).

This is a personality assessment designed to screen out candidates who may engage in counterproductive work behaviors. It is not an IQ test; it is a risk-assessment tool used to determine if a candidate has the temperament and reliability required for policing.

What is it Measuring?
The ESQ2 focuses on predicting "counterproductive work behaviors." In a policing context, this is critical because the cost of error is high. The test evaluates candidates across several dimensions to flag potential risks in areas such as:

Lateness and Absenteeism: Are you reliable? Do you show up on time?

Safety Violations: Do you take unnecessary risks or ignore safety protocols?

Driving Delinquency: Do you have a history of aggressive or careless driving?

Unauthorized Breaks/Loafing: Do you waste time or avoid work?

Customer Service Issues: Are you rude, dismissive, or argumentative with the public?

THE STRUCTURE OF THE TEST

Format: Multiple-choice questionnaire (e.g., True/False or Agree/Disagree scales).

Length: Typically takes about 15–20 minutes to complete.

Type of Questions: You will see statements about your past behaviors, your attitudes toward work, and your reactions to hypothetical situations.

Examples of Typical Themes:

"I sometimes lose my temper when things don't go my way."

"It is okay to take small items from work if no one notices."

"I am never late for appointments."

The "Lie Detector" Scale (Faking Good)
One of the most critical aspects of the ESQ2 is its built-in validity scales. The test is designed to catch candidates who are trying to "game" the system by answering how they think a police officer should answer, rather than how they actually feel.

This is often called the Social Desirability Scale.

If you answer "False" to a statement like "I have sometimes told a lie to get out of trouble" or "I have gossiped about a coworker," the test may flag you. Why? Because everyone has done these things at some point. Claiming you are perfect suggests dishonesty or a lack of self-awareness.

The Golden Rule: If you try to appear perfect, you will likely fail the validity check.

Strategies for Success

1. Be Honest, but Professional
You must be truthful, but you should answer from your "best self" perspective—the version of you that shows up to work, not the version of you relaxing on a Saturday night with friends.

> **Avoid absolutes:** Be wary of words like "Never" or "Always." Very few things in human behavior are absolute.
>
> **Own your flaws (within reason):** Admitting to minor, universal human failings (like occasionally being late or getting frustrated) makes you look honest. Admitting to major red flags (like stealing or chronic safety violations) will hurt your score.

2. Consistency is Key
The test will ask similar questions in different ways to see if your answers remain consistent.

Question A: "I enjoy following strict rules."

Question B: "I prefer to make my own rules rather than follow instructions." If you answer "Agree" to A and "Agree" to B, the test will flag the inconsistency. Read every question carefully.

3. Don't Overthink It
These tests are designed to be taken quickly. If you spend 2 minutes agonizing over a single question, you are likely over-analyzing the hidden meaning. Go with your gut instinct, keeping your professional "work persona" in mind.

4. Understand the "Police Personality"
While there is no single "police personality," agencies generally look for candidates who are:

Conscientious: Organized, dependable, and disciplined.

Emotionally Stable: Calm under pressure and not easily angered.

Agreeable: Cooperative and able to work within a team structure.

Open to Experience: Willing to learn new things (though in policing, this is balanced with a respect for tradition/protocol).

Sample Personality Questions & Analysis

Note: The following are examples designed to illustrate the logic behind personality testing. The actual ESQ2 will contain different specific statements, but the underlying themes will be similar.

Example 1: The "Saint" Trap (Validity Scale)
Statement: "I have never told a lie in my entire life."
Options: Strongly Disagree | Disagree | Neutral | Agree | Strongly Agree

Analysis: This is a classic "validity" question designed to catch candidates who are "faking good."
The Trap: You might think, "Police officers must be honest, so I must say I never lie."
The Reality: Everyone has told a lie at some point (e.g., a white lie to spare someone's feelings). Claiming you never lie is statistically impossible for a human adult.

Best Approach: Acknowledging this statement as "False" (or Disagreeing) shows you are honest about your own humanity. Answering "Strongly Agree" flags you as someone trying too hard to look perfect.

Example 2: Authority & Rules (Conscientiousness)
Statement: "Sometimes it is necessary to ignore the rules to get the job done quickly."

Options: Strongly Disagree | Disagree | Neutral | Agree | Strongly Agree

Analysis: This measures your Safety Orientation and Conscientiousness.

The Trap: In some industries, "getting it done" is rewarded over protocol.

The Reality: In policing, "ignoring rules" can lead to evidence being thrown out of court, safety hazards, or liability lawsuits. Speed is rarely more important than legality and safety.

Best Approach: Disagreement is key here. A police service needs to know that you respect procedure, even when it is inconvenient.

Example 3: Emotional Control (Stability)
Statement: "I tend to hold a grudge when someone insults me."

Options: Strongly Disagree | Disagree | Neutral | Agree | Strongly Agree

Analysis: This measures Emotional Stability and Forgiveness.

The Trap: You might feel it's natural to be angry when insulted.
The Reality: Police officers are insulted frequently by the public. If you hold grudges or internalize insults, you are a high risk for burnout or excessive force.

Best Approach: Disagreement. You want to demonstrate that you have "thick skin" and can let negative interactions roll off your back without carrying that anger into your next call.

Example 4: Work Ethic (Reliability)
Statement: "If my supervisor isn't watching, I sometimes take extra-long breaks."

Options: Strongly Disagree | Disagree | Neutral | Agree | Strongly Agree

Analysis: This measures Integrity and Productivity.

The Trap: This is a straightforward admission of counter-productive behavior.

The Reality: Policing is often autonomous (you are alone in a patrol car). The agency needs to know you will work hard without constant supervision.

Best Approach: Strongly Disagree. This touches on core integrity. Unlike "I never lie" (which is impossible), "I never steal time from my employer" is a standard you can and should meet.

Example 5: Teamwork (Agreeableness)
Statement: "I prefer to work alone rather than as part of a group."

Options: Strongly Disagree | Disagree | Neutral | Agree | Strongly Agree

Analysis: This measures Social Preference and Team Orientation.

The Trap: You might genuinely be an introvert.

The Reality: While officers are often in a car alone, they are part of a tight-knit squad and must rely on backup. A "lone wolf" mentality can be dangerous.

Best Approach: Leaning toward disagreement. You don't have to be the life of the party, but you must demonstrate a willingness and ability to function within a unit.

SUMMARY CHECKLIST FOR CANDIDATES

When you sit down to take the ESQ2, keep this mental checklist in mind:

☑ Is this a "Saint" question? (Am I claiming to be perfect? -> Be honest/human.)

☑ Is this a "Safety" question? (Am I risking safety for speed? -> Choose Safety.)

☑ Is this a "Stability" question? (Am I getting angry/anxious? -> Choose Calm.)

☑ Is this an "Integrity" question? (Am I stealing time/items? -> Choose Integrity.)

THE 14-DAY FITNESS LOG

While the SIGMA Survey tests your mind, the 14-Day Fitness Log is the first test of your discipline and integrity.
As part of the OACP Certificate process, you are required to submit a completed log detailing your physical activity for 14 consecutive days. This document is mandatory. You cannot receive your OACP Certificate without it.

Many candidates treat this as a "check-the-box" exercise, but recruiters and adjudicators review these logs to assess two things:

> **1. Physical Readiness:** Are you maintaining a lifestyle that will allow you to pass the physical testing (shuttle run, circuit, etc.) later in the process?
>
> **2. Integrity & Attention to Detail:** Can you follow instructions and document daily events accurately?

Fitness Log

Why is the Fitness Log Required?
Policing is a physically demanding profession. The OACP (Ontario Association of Chiefs of Police) requires evidence that you are already living an active lifestyle before you even apply.

The log proves that fitness is a habit for you, not just something you cram for the night before a test. It serves as a "good faith" declaration that you are physically prepared to attend the Ontario Police College.

Rules for the Fitness Log

To ensure your log is accepted, follow these "Golden Rules":

1. Consecutive Days: You must track 14 days in a row. You cannot skip weekends or days you were "too busy."

2. **Honesty is Mandatory:** Do not fabricate workouts. If you had a rest day, mark it as a rest day (but explain what you did for active recovery, like stretching). Falsifying this document is an integrity breach and grounds for disqualification.

3. **Variety:** A log that lists "Walking the dog - 20 mins" for 14 days straight may be technically accurate, but it does not demonstrate the physical readiness required for police work. Your log should show a mix of cardiovascular training and strength training.

How to Fill Out the Log

The standard OACP Fitness Log generally asks for three main details per entry: Activity, Duration, and Intensity.

1. Activity

Be specific. Vague entries look suspicious or lazy.

- Bad: "Gym" or "Workout."
- Good: "5km Run (Treadmill)" or "Strength Training (Chest and Triceps)."

2. Duration

Record the time spent actively exercising. Do not include travel time to the gym or time spent chatting in the locker room.

- **Format:** Minutes (e.g., "45 mins").

3. Intensity

You need to describe how hard you worked. You can use a descriptive word (Low, Moderate, High) or the RPE Scale (Rate of Perceived Exertion) from 1 to 10.

- Low (RPE 1-3): Easy conversation, no sweating. (e.g., Walking, Stretching).
- Moderate (RPE 4-6): Breathing heavier, light sweat, can still talk but not sing. (e.g., Jogging, light weights).
- High (RPE 7-10): Heavy breathing, profuse sweating, cannot hold a conversation. (e.g., Sprints, heavy lifting, HIIT).

Sample Entries: Good vs. Bad

Your log needs to look professional. Here is a comparison of how to write your entries.

Date	Poor Entry (Avoid)	Good Entry
Day 1	Went for a run.	Cardio: 5km outdoor run. Time: 30 mins. Intensity: High.
Day 2	Lifted weights.	Strength: Upper body (Bench press, rows, shoulder press). Time: 45 mins. Intensity: Moderate/High.
Day 3	Rest.	Active Recovery: 20 min Yoga/Stretching routine. Intensity: Low.
Day 4	Played sports	Cardio/Agility: Pickup basketball game. Time: 60 mins. Intensity: High (intervals).

Common Questions

Q: Can I have Rest Days?
A: Yes. Rest is essential for training. However, you should aim to have "Active Recovery" rather than "doing nothing." Stretching, foam rolling, or a light walk are great entries for a rest day. A log with 7 rest days out of 14 will likely be flagged as insufficient.

Q: What if I get sick during the 14 days?
A: If you are ill, you should stop the log and restart when you are healthy. Submitting a log where you did nothing for 5 days due to the flu does not help your application. Restart the 14-day count when you are back on your feet.

Q: Does walking my dog count?
A: It counts as "activity," but it should not be your only source of fitness. Police work requires anaerobic power (sprinting/fighting) and strength. Walking is aerobic and low intensity. If you list walking, try to pair it with a bodyweight circuit (pushups/sit-ups).

5 Tips for a "Gold Standard" Log

1. **Print Legibly:** If you are filling it out by hand, write clearly. If the adjudicator can't read it, they can't pass it. (Ideally, type it into the PDF form if allowed).

2. **Include the Shuttle Run:** Since you will eventually have to run the Beep Test (Leger Shuttle Run) for the police agencies, try to include at least one practice session of the Shuttle Run in your 14-day log. It shows you are proactive.

3. **Balance Cardio and Strength:** Aim for a 50/50 split. Policing requires both the ability to chase (cardio) and the ability to control a suspect (strength).

4. Be Consistent: Try to exercise at the same time of day if possible. It shows routine and discipline.

5. Review Before Submitting: Check for spelling errors. Yes, even in a fitness log! "Bicep Curls" is correct; "Bicep Curls" is not. Attention to detail matters.

Summary

The 14-Day Fitness Log is your opportunity to show the OACP that you are self-motivated. You don't need a gym membership to pass this requirement—bodyweight exercises (push-ups, lunges, burpees) and running are perfectly acceptable. Just ensure you record them with detail, accuracy, and honesty.

MEDICAL STANDARDS

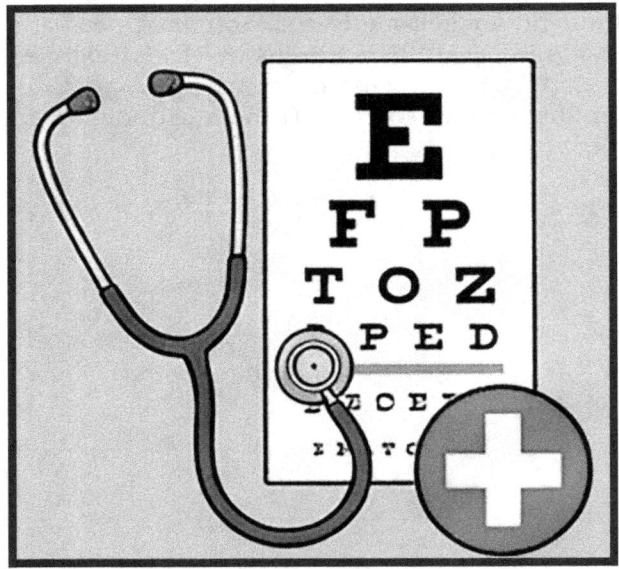

While the SIGMA tests your mind and the Fitness Log tracks your habits, the Medical Examination assesses your biological readiness for duty.

Police work is physically dangerous and biologically demanding. Officers work rotating shifts, drive at high speeds, and must be able to physically intervene in volatile situations. For these reasons, the OACP (Ontario Association of Chiefs of Police) has established strict medical standards that all applicants must meet to ensure they are not a danger to themselves, their partners, or the public.

This chapter breaks down the "Big Three" medical hurdles: Vision, Hearing, and General Health.

Medical Standards

1. How the Medical Process Works
Unlike the online aptitude tests, the medical assessment is completed by your own healthcare providers.1

> **1. Download the Package:** When you register for the OACP Certificate, you will receive a "Medical Examination Package" (PDF).
>
> **2. Book Your Appointments:** You must take this package to:
> - An Optometrist or Ophthalmologist (for vision).
> - An Audiologist or Hearing Instrument Specialist (for hearing).2
>
> **3. The Sign-Off:** These specialists will test you against the specific OACP standards and sign the forms.
>
> **4. Submission:** You do not submit these results to the OACP certificate firm. You submit them directly to the Police Service you are applying to (e.g., Toronto Police, OPP, Peel) alongside your application.

Important: These forms are generally valid for 2 years.3 If your medical clearance expires during your application process, you may need to pay to have them redone.

2. Vision Standards
Vision is the most common medical stumbling block for applicants. Police officers must be able to identify license plates, read descriptions, and see clearly in low-light environments—sometimes without their glasses (e.g., if they are knocked off in a struggle).

The "Uncorrected" Rule
The most confusing standard for candidates is Uncorrected Visual Acuity. This measures how well you can see without glasses or contacts.

Even if you have 20/20 vision with your glasses on, you can still be disqualified if your vision without them is too poor.

Laser Eye Surgery (LASIK / PRK)
If you do not meet the "Uncorrected" standard (20/40), you may need corrective laser eye surgery.

- **The Wait Period:** You generally must wait 30 days after surgery before you can be medically cleared.

- **The Form:** Your surgeon must complete a specific section of the medical package confirming your vision is stable and you have no side effects (like halos or night blindness).

3. Hearing Standards

Hearing loss is often undetectable in normal conversation but can be critical when listening to radio transmissions over the sound of a siren.

The Decibel (dB) Standard

You will undergo an Audiogram. The specialist will play tones at different frequencies (pitch) and volumes.

What if I fail the Audiogram?

If you fail the initial beep test, you are not automatically disqualified. You can request a Stage 2 Test called the HINT (Hearing in Noise Test). This tests your ability to understand spoken words with background noise. Many candidates who fail the pure-tone test pass the HINT.

4. General Medical Restrictions

Beyond eyes and ears, you will eventually undergo a full physical by a physician designated by the hiring police service.

They look for conditions that could cause "Sudden Incapacitation" (fainting, seizure, coma) or inability to perform duties.

Common Conditions & Rules

- **Seizure Disorders (Epilepsy):** Generally, you must be seizure-free for a specific period (often 1 to 5 years depending on the service) without the use of medication. If you require medication to stop seizures, you may be disqualified due to the risk of missing a dose during extended shifts.

- **Diabetes:** Type 1 and Type 2 diabetics can be hired, provided they can demonstrate stability. You may need to provide a history of A1C levels and a letter from your specialist confirming you are not prone to severe hypoglycemic episodes.
- **Heart Conditions:** Any condition that limits physical exertion (e.g., uncorrected heart murmur, history of heart attack) will require a review by a cardiologist.

The "Social Media Audit" Checklist

Your resume gets you the interview. Your social media gets you disqualified.

In the age of digital policing, background investigators are not just calling your references; they are digital detectives. Before you submit your application to any police service in Ontario (or Saskatoon), you must conduct a ruthless audit of your digital footprint.

Recruiters are looking for Character, Judgment, and Integrity. A post glorifying drug use, a racist meme shared "as a joke," or a video of you driving at excessive speeds proves you lack the judgment required to carry a badge and a gun.

The "Grandmother Rule"

Before we get to the checklist, apply this simple heuristic to every single post, photo, and comment:

"Would I be comfortable projecting this image on a screen in a room full of my grandmother, the Chief of Police, and a judge?"

If the answer is "No" or even "Maybe," delete it.

Part 1: The General Search

Before you log into your accounts, see what the public sees.

- ✅ The Google Test: Open an "Incognito" or "Private" browser window. Search your full name, your nickname, and your email address.
- o Look for: Old blogs, forum posts, or news articles you forgot about.
- ✅ The Image Search: Click the "Images" tab on Google after searching your name.
- o Look for: Photos from old sports teams or parties that are hosted on other people's websites.
- ✅ The Handle Check: Do you use the same username (e.g., CoolGuy99) across multiple sites? Search that username. It might link your professional LinkedIn to your anonymous Reddit account.

Part 2: Profile Hygiene (All Platforms)

- ✅ Professional Handles: If your Instagram or Twitter handle is Partyanimal_24/7 or contains profanity, change it. Use your name or something neutral.
- ✅ Email Addresses: Ensure the email on your resume is professional (e.g., firstname.lastname@gmail.com), not sexybeast88@hotmail.com.
- ✅ Profile Photos: Your profile picture should be clear and respectable.
- o Remove: Photos with alcohol (even red solo cups), middle fingers, gang signs, or revealing swimwear.

☑ Bios: Check your bio text. Remove aggressive quotes, political manifestos, or emojis that could be misinterpreted (e.g., the syringe, the pill, or gun emojis).

Part 3: The Content Deep Dive

You need to scroll back. All the way back. Investigators know that you behave differently now than you did at 16, but they will still look at your history to judge your maturation.

Facebook

☑ **The "About" Section:** Check your "Likes," "Movies," and "Books." Did you "Like" a page called "I hate cops" or "Legalize It" 10 years ago? Unlike them immediately.

☑ **Tagged Photos:** This is the most dangerous section. You might not have posted the photo of you passing out at a keg party, but if your friend tagged you, it's on your profile.

o **Action:** Untag yourself and ask the friend to delete it.

☑ **Timeline Review:** Scroll back to your high school years. Delete the teenage drama, the bullying, and the immature rants.

Instagram / TikTok

☑ **The Content:** Does your feed suggest a lifestyle of fitness, community, and family? Or does it suggest narcissism, partying, and recklessness?

☑ **Stories:** Remember that while Stories disappear, people can screenshot them. Be mindful of what you post on weekends.

☑ **Following:** Who do you follow? If you follow accounts known for hate speech, radical political violence, or illegal street racing, you are guilty by association. Unfollow them.

X (formerly Twitter)

☑ **The "Replies" Tab:** Investigators love this tab. You might not tweet offensive things, but did you get into an argument with a stranger and use racial or homophobic slurs?
　　o　　**Action:** Search your own handle + specific bad words to find and delete these old interactions.

☑ **Retweets:** A Retweet is an endorsement. If you retweeted controversial political conspiracy theories, delete them.

Part 4: The "Private" Account Myth

"My account is private, so I'm safe." False.

1. **The "Log-In" Request:** During a background interview or home visit, a recruiter may ask you to pull up your social media on your phone and scroll through it with them. You cannot hide behind a privacy setting then.

2. **The "Friend of a Friend":** Police officers are everywhere. If you have 500 followers, chances are one of them knows a cop. Screenshots leak.

Part 5: The "Red Flag" Keywords
Scan your history for these instant disqualifiers:

- **Drug References:** Jokes about "420," "munchies," or photos with paraphernalia.
- **Excessive Alcohol:** Photos of binge drinking, funneling beer, or being visibly intoxicated.
- **Bigotry:** ANY use of the N-word, homophobic slurs, or derogatory terms for women, even if it was "lyrics to a song" or "just a joke with friends." This is often a zero-tolerance automatic fail.
- **Anti-Police Sentiment:** "F*** the Police" posts (FTP), or support for movements that advocate violence against law enforcement.
- **Sexual Content:** Soliciting sex, "Thirst traps," or OnlyFans links.

SUMMARY

When in doubt, DELETE.
You are applying for a job that requires the public's trust. If your social media suggests you cannot be trusted to represent the Service with dignity, you will not be hired. It is better to have a boring social media profile than an exciting one that costs you your career.

Conclusion

Congratulations! You have made it to the end. By finishing this guide, you have shown the discipline and dedication required for a successful career in law enforcement.

Passing this test is the first step toward securing and building a rewarding future. You have put in the work—now trust your preparation.

Study. Practice. Succeed. We are rooting for you!

Don't Stop Now – Get Free Extras We want to make sure you are fully prepared. Register your copy to access free updates, additional test tips, and bonus practice questions.

Claim your extras here:

https://www.test-preparation.ca/register/

Online Resources

How to Prepare for a Test - The Ultimate Guide
https://www.test-preparation.ca/prepare-test/

Learning Styles - The Complete Guide
https://www.test-preparation.ca/learning-style/

Test Anxiety Secrets!
https://www.test-preparation.ca/test-anxiety/

Time Management on a Test
https://www.test-preparation.ca/time-management/

Flash Cards - The Complete Guide
https://www.test-preparation.ca/flash-cards/

How to Memorize - The Complete Guide
https://www.test-preparation.ca/memorize/

www.ingramcontent.com/pod-product-compliance
Lightning Source LLC
Chambersburg PA
CBHW072013070526
44583CB00015B/1460